# CABLE NEWS
## CONFIDENTIAL

# CABLE NEWS
# CONFIDENTIAL

## My Misadventures in Corporate Media

### JEFF COHEN

#### FOREWORD BY JIM HIGHTOWER

PoliPointPress

This edition published in 2006 in the United States of America by PoliPointPress, P.O. Box 3008, Sausalito, CA 94966
www.p3books.com

Production management: Michael Bass Associates
Cover design: Jeff Kenyon
Cover image: Holger Scheibe/zefa/Corbis

Library of Congress Cataloging-In-Publication Data

Cohen, Jeff
Cable News Confidential: My Misadventures in Corporate Media | Jeff Cohen | foreword by Jim Hightower

ISBN: 0-9760621-6-X

Library of Congress Control Number: 2006901819

Printed in the United States of America
June 2006

Published by:
PoliPointPress, LLC
P.O. Box 3008
Sausalito, CA 94966-3008
(415) 339-4100
www.p3books.com

Distributed by Publishers Group West

*Dedicated to the thousands of conscientious journalists who toil on behalf of an informed public—whether in independent media or inside the corporate media colossus.*

# CONTENTS

# CONTENTS

## PART THREE: MSNBC

# FOREWORD

## JIM HIGHTOWER

Sheesh, cable news. So much potential, so much waste. It takes only a couple of facts to sum up the sorry state of this journalistic medium:

- The most credible anchor in all of cableland is on Comedy Central.

- The loopiest person on cable is not Bill O'Reilly, even though he routinely goes on such rightwing rants as calling for terrorists to attack San Francisco ("You want to blow up the Coit Tower? Go ahead."). Despite such spite, he's still several notches lower on the wacky gauge than Ann Coulter, who regularly explodes with such bile as calling Democrats like decorated war veteran John Murtha "gutless traitors" who "long to see U.S. troops shot." She's loopier than a Coney Island whirligig.

It's not the on-air whackos, however, who make cable news such a gross disappointment. That credit must be pinned to the lapels of the Suits who own and run it—Time Warner (CNN), News Corporation (Fox) and General Electric (MSNBC).

Cable television began as an exciting opportunity to provide an independent, informative and irreverent look at the news—supported by viewer subscriptions and perhaps freer of advertiser pressure. Today, it has devolved to just another conglomerate product whose managers stay focused on the corporate bottom line, practicing a timid journalism dedicated to being as inoffensive as possible to the established order. Mavericks need not apply.

But years ago, media critic Jeff Cohen applied for cable entry and actually got in. Jeff is the very definition of the term *Media Maverick*, yet for more than a decade, this outsider had an on-again/off-again feisty career inside CNN, Fox and MSNBC before his final ouster by the Suits in 2003. This book is his personal chronicle of "The Adventures of Jeff in Cableland." Or "A Media Critic Goes Behind Enemy Lines."

The crucial message that unfolds, juicy-bit by juicy-bit, in the following pages is that our so-called political leaders (Democrats as well as Republicans) have failed miserably in their obligation to see to it that our publicly-owned airwaves are used for We the People. Instead, politicians—corrupted by the campaign donations of broadcast barons (who also happen to control a politician's access to news and talk shows)—have allowed a handful of moneyed elites to privatize our media and control America's televised dialogue.

This gives them the power not only to determine what's on the air but also to keep important news and viewpoints off the air. As Jeff reveals in firsthand detail, a dangerous example of this narrowing of our democracy's essential public debate came in the run-up to Bush's war in Iraq. Cable news was especially offensive, with managers all but dressing their reporters in cheerleading skirts and having them wave pom-poms at George W.'s misguided adventure. Nothing that politicians do is more serious than committing our men and women (and our nation's reputation) to bloody combat. Yet, cable's "newscasters" rarely reflected the vibrant debate going on in our country over the war—or the extent of active and organized dissent.

★   ★   ★

Those of us who bemoan the corporate takeover of TV and radio cannot drown our sorrows in a glass of whine. Don't agonize—organize. First, we must recognize that we've been here before. Periodically in America's history, the media barons of the day have ignored or trivialized vital democratic movements—but the people fought back.

Beginning in the 1870s, for example, the fast-spreading populist movement of tenant farmers, urban laborers and grassroots reformers found themselves up against the recalcitrant press establishment of the Robber Barons. They were blocked from mass-market coverage of their ideas and actions, but rather than wringing their hands, these scrappy rebels joined hands and began reaching the public through media of their own creation. This included a network of more than 1,000 newspapers (the Reform Press Association), such large-circulation magazines as the *National Economist* and the *American Nonconformist*, and a speaker's bureau of 40,000 trained lecturers who on any given night could spread out across the countryside and bring home the true news of the day.

So here we are, 130 years or so down the road from the populists, up against the latest manifestation of concentrated media power. Shall we wring our hands—or join hands? The good news, as Jeff points out in his uplifting epilogue, is that folks all across the country are joining hands. They are creating a thoroughly-progressive, mass-market media through websites, podcasts, blogs, TV, radio, weekly papers, newsletters, public speeches, books, movies, theater, songs, art, discussion networks, coffee klatches, potlucks, beer nights, knitting clubs, carrier pigeons, smoke signals and anything else they can think of to spread the word.

Added together, these outlets reach millions of people every day. Progressives have the makings of a powerful media network. It's up to us. My momma told me long ago that two wrongs don't make a right—but I soon figured out that three left turns do! Just as others have done before us, we can put our creative heads together and figure how to get around the corporate media barons.

As Jeff's inside report makes clear, creating a new media for our democracy is not something we might do, could do, should do—but must do. This is a *big* time for America. Corporate elites have enthroned themselves to rule not only our airwaves but also our economy and government, supplanting our democracy with their plutocracy.

People know this. Most Americans say our country is "headed in the wrong direction." Even more Americans say that government serves corporate power rather than people like them. Public approval of politicians is down at about the approval level of mad cow disease. The only ones ranked lower than politicians are the media.

People everywhere—in red states as well as blue—yearn to have an open, honest, democratic discussion about the rise of corporate supremacy and how to take our country back. Let's begin with the media. Jeff Cohen's book is a clarion call for you to join this historic fight.

*Don't wanna be an American idiot.*
*One nation controlled by the media.*
—Green Day

# INTRODUCTION
## EMBEDDED

October 12, 1999—Gen. Pervez Musharraf seizes power in Pakistan in a military coup. India, twice in open war with Pakistan over the disputed province of Kashmir, puts its military on high alert. The nations have exchanged heavy artillery fire for months, and India blames Musharraf for the bloodshed. With Pakistan's recent A-bomb test, the so-called "Islamic bomb," both nations are now armed with the ultimate weapon. Tensions mount, and a nuclear exchange suddenly becomes thinkable.

Three days later, I slide into my chair at Fox News as a pundit on the weekly show *News Watch*, one of the smarter programs on cable news. As the world hangs on developments from the nuclear tinder box, the "we report/you decide" network cuts straight to the essentials:

- JonBenet Ramsey, the 6-year-old beauty pageant winner murdered in Colorado, gets six minutes and our entire opening segment.

- O.J. Simpson, in the news again because of a domestic dispute with his girlfriend in Florida, consumes our second segment.

- In our third and final discussion segment, we chew over an NBC *Law and Order* episode in which a character used the term "Lewinsky" as a synonym for a sex act.

Pakistan? India? Nuclear war? Never mentioned.

As I walk out of the studio, my brain jumps back to the ironic 1980s-era bumper sticker: *One Nuclear Bomb Can Ruin Your Whole Day.*

1

But I want it updated for today's cable TV news:

*One Nuclear Bomb Can Ruin Your Whole Day . . .*
*But Who Cares? O.J.'s Back in the News.*

★  ★  ★

Welcome to the breathless, wheezing world of 24-hour cable television news. They're called "news channels," but "reality-based entertainment channels" is more like it. Some call them "infotainment" channels; I prefer the label "disinfotainment."

A moment ago, I described *Fox News Watch* as "one of the smarter programs on cable news." That's a high jump over a low hurdle.

The intellectual level of cable news is one step above pro wrestling. There's an old joke: *What do pro wrestling and the U.S. Senate have in common? Both are dominated by overweight white guys pretending to hurt each other.* Cable news is dominated by overcoifed white guys pretending to hurt each other. Overcaffeinated, too.

I know cable news better than I ever wanted to. I started appearing as a guest on CNN in the 1980s when it was the only news channel on cable. But CNN attracted competitors, as others saw how easy and relatively cheap it could be to spatter "news" across 24 hours. Over the years, I've been a pundit on all three such channels: I got my feet wet at CNN (1987–1996), waded halfway in at Fox News (1997–2002), and became completely submerged at MSNBC (2002–2003), where I was a senior producer and on-air contributor.

This book describes what I found inside cable news: a drunken exuberance for sex, crime and celebrity stories, matched by a grim timidity and fear of offending the powers-that-be—especially if the powers-that-be are conservatives. The biggest fear is of doing anything that could get you, or your network, accused of being liberal.

I also found in cable news a passion for following the media pack (sometimes resembling a lynch mob)—whether in pursuit of a sex scandal or war. And a fear of finding yourself alone, asking questions no one else is asking.

Cable news is in the business of entertainment, using traditional Hollywood genres to attract viewers: lurid crime drama (O.J., JonBenet, Laci Peterson), sex farce (Clinton/Lewinsky), suspense thriller (Beltway sniper), war (with special theme music and graphics).

It's news as soap opera—anything to grab an audience, or a sliver of an audience . . . especially if it can be done cheaply. While over 25 million people typically watch the nightly news on the three major broadcast networks, the three cable news channels are thrilled when they can ride a crime or sex story to expand their typical 3 million combined primetime viewers to 5 or

GETTING "LEWINSKIED"

Nuclear tensions rise; we talk sex on Fox.

6 million. Imagine Bill O'Reilly's mixed emotions when his ratings soared at Fox News after he himself was sued for sexual harassment.

Once upon a time, TV news put journalists on camera. Today, cable news has on-air "talent"—who are "cast," not just hired. A Walter Cronkite would have big trouble getting a job today in TV news. But an actor? No problem. CNN a few years ago cast a former actress from *NYPD Blue* as one of its Headline News anchors. At Fox News, where lip gloss and blond hair go further than a background in journalism, I could find no proof to the charge that executives reviewed audition tapes of potential female anchors with the sound turned off.*

★ ★ ★

Despite its relatively small audience, cable news is influential among the political class—journalists, officials, operatives, activists—in framing debates and anointing stars. But many politicos are frustrated by the drift in cable news from politics to tabloid and fluff. I happened to be in a CNN greenroom years ago when Texas senator Phil Gramm nearly jumped out of his chair at seeing scantily clad models traversing a runway on CNN's fashion program, *Style with Elsa Klensch*. "Id dat CNN?" yelped Gramm in disbelief. "Id dat really CNN?!"

---

*In 2001, when Hollywood TV executive Jamie Kellner became CEO of CNN's parent, Turner Broadcasting, he referred to staff changes at CNN as "casting" changes; the actress was soon hired for "star power." In an email, Kellner's lieutenant said that CNN needs "younger, more attractive anchors." CNN hired Paula Zahn months later and promoted her in an ad as "sexy," with a sound effect that seemed to resemble a zipper unzipping.

Phil Gramm and fashion models might seem like an odd mix, but not in the motley stew of cable news. When Gramm ran for president in 1996, he repeatedly framed his major challenge as whether "someone so ugly can be elected president." Apparently not—suggesting limits to the old adage about politics being show business for ugly people. Cable news has its limits as well: while someone like Sen. Gramm could be a semi-regular guest, no one would cast him as an anchor. A fashion model was more likely.

★   ★   ★

My path to cable news was roundabout—and I carried a sizeable chip on my shoulder the whole way. Quite simply: TV news could have gotten me killed. At age 15, I was a gung-ho Vietnam War hawk whose views on the war were totally shaped by my avid consumption of network TV news. I wrote a school paper condemning football star Joe Namath, whose bad knee kept him out of Vietnam but not off the gridiron every Sunday. "Namath is healthy enough to play one of the roughest sports on earth," I fumed, "but not to defend his country in Vietnam."

Defend his country by attacking a peasant society in Asia that couldn't hurt us if it wanted to? I admit it: my views were a bit wacked. But no more so than millions of other Americans who got their pre-1968 news about Vietnam from television. Or the millions who got their news in 2002 about Iraq's WMD from cable news . . . but that jumps ahead of our story.

Thankfully, before reaching draft age, I started learning about Vietnam from magazines like *Harper's* and *Ramparts* and by talking to returning Vietnam veterans. I became a peace activist. In my hometown of Detroit in 1971, I had a life-changing experience at the Winter Soldier hearings organized by Vietnam vets to present testimony about the horrors they'd seen and the atrocities against Vietnamese they'd witnessed or participated in. Many vets blamed media propaganda for deceiving them into going to Vietnam in the first place.

The powerful, emotional testimony from vets on the realities of Vietnam could have turned many Americans against the war, but few major U.S. media covered the event. When a rare mainstream camera crew abruptly packed up and departed in the middle of particularly riveting testimony, a roomful of vets jeered and booed. It was the moment I became a media critic. I was 19.

I borrowed my dad's car to attend the Winter Soldier hearings and many other antiwar and civil rights events around Detroit at the time. As a result, the Michigan State Police "intelligence unit" started keeping a dossier on . . . my dad. The bumbling spies traced his license plate and assumed that the "subversive" in our family, the one helping Vietnam Veterans Against the War, was Sol Cohen. But Sol was no card-carrying activist; the only cards he ever carried were Visa and American Express.

Years later, a judge put the Michigan spy unit out of business and ordered release of all surveillance files to the 38,000 lawful activists who'd been monitored—including elected officials, union leaders, feminists and civil rights advocates. As a proud activist, I was crushed to learn there was no dossier on me—just the subversive file on my dad, the kind of upright, hardworking, small businessman our society is supposed to cherish.

As I say, Sol Cohen was no radical. In 1972, he fired me from his clothing store over my union activities: "You're a wonderful dad," I quipped. "But a class enemy."

At age 23, I moved to Los Angeles to attend the Peoples College of Law, a leftish law school where students cleaned the toilets, hired the professors, and pretty much ran the place. This was not your typical competitive law school—PCL had no dean's list. It didn't even have a dean. It was the only law school where an arrest record actually helped you gain admission—think of it as "affirmative action for civil disobedients."

I worked my way through school as a freelance journalist and activist, exposing police brutality and political spying by the LAPD and FBI. In that era, criticizing the cops prompted retaliation. My tennis partner, I would learn years later, was a full-time LAPD undercover agent assigned to spy on me and my friends. She apparently had a crush on me. Fortunately, it wasn't mutual.

After graduation, the ACLU Foundation of Southern California hired me as a junior lawyer to work on a massive First Amendment lawsuit against the City of Los Angeles over the actions of my former tennis partner and a dozen other undercover spies. We unearthed documents showing that the LAPD had taken notes on the political activities of Rev. Jesse Jackson, farmworker leader César Chávez, Stevie Wonder, Jackson Browne—not to mention the black mayor of Los Angeles and thousands of other law-abiding citizens.

I recall only one actual terrorist's name surfacing in the course of our suit against the LAPD's so-called "anti-terrorism" unit—Donald "Cinque" DeFreeze, who led the tiny gang that kidnapped heiress Patricia Hearst in 1974. But he wasn't a target of surveillance. A police supervisor admitted to me under oath that DeFreeze had himself been an LAPD undercover informant prior to forming his "Liberation Army"—history largely unknown about the alleged revolutionary.

Our ever-expanding suit was heading toward trial just as journalists from around the globe were preparing to head to Los Angeles for the 1984 Olympics. The whole world would be watching. To avert an embarrassing trial, the city offered us stricter surveillance rules and a $1.8 million settlement. We said yes. I received some cash as both an attorney and a plaintiff in the case.

FAIR's first protest, KABC-TV in L.A.

It was then—after my first case—that I retired from the legal profession. Few lawyers can say they never lost a case . . . or say so honestly.

What would I do now? I had a little money and a lot of free time. And I still had that chip on my shoulder about the mainstream media. With the help of friends and a few dollars left from the LAPD suit, I moved to New York in 1986 to launch the media-watch group FAIR (Fairness & Accuracy In Reporting). We set out to document bias (especially in who speaks and who doesn't in mainstream news), expose corporate censorship and advocate for minority and dissenting voices. Over time, we won the respect of more than a few mainstream journalists.

FAIR's main goal was to take progressive media criticism out of the ghetto of small publications and propel it into the biggest media outlets we could access. As FAIR's founder and director, it was part of my job to appear—as frequently as possible—on national TV. Thanks to round-the-clock cable news, that came easier than anyone expected.

★ ★ ★

I never intended a career in cable news. Even more unlikely than blow-dried reporters embedded inside the U.S. Army, I was a media critic who became embedded inside mainstream TV news. At FAIR, I was a vociferous critic of TV news. An outsider. The guy who cast the first stone at the glass studios. But I soon found myself in a slow-motion Alice-in-Wonderland nightmare: Instead of falling into a rabbit hole, I fell into the hot, fetid soup of cable news.

When I lived in L.A., my pal and I were regulars at Norm's 24-hour restaurants, where the menu beckoned customers to ask about the soup du jour in Norm's "steaming tureen." My buddy thought it was a hoot to see the varied reactions on waitresses' faces when he'd earnestly ask, "What's the soup today in your steaming latrine?"

That's cable news nowadays . . . more steaming latrine than steaming tureen.

As a media critic, I had long denounced the takeover of the news business by a half-dozen giant conglomerates with financial interests in everything from weaponry to nuclear plants to amusement parks. These half-dozen corporations, I'd complained, were constricting journalism—sitting on the windpipe of the First Amendment. By now I've taken a check from half those companies.

The most delicious thing about my TV career was that I was able to denounce the biggest media in America—on cable channels owned by the biggest media in America. Throughout my years as a paid pundit, I was a firm believer in biting the hands that fed me. Not until this book did I have a chance to make a full-course meal of them.

★ ★ ★

You say you don't watch television. You don't even own a TV. You killed your TV. Here's news for you: TV is alive and well in your neighbors' homes. Despite the amazing growth of the Internet, it remains our country's dominant medium, especially during war, crisis and election.

For me, my tenure in TV news was an intense learning experience. For you, the reader, I hope it offers a window into an opinion-shaping medium of unrivaled influence.

After getting inside, I was no longer just a media critic carping at the content on the TV screen, but one who knew something about how that content was cooked up. I was like a restaurant critic who gained access to the most closely guarded kitchens and stayed around long enough for the chefs to forget I was there . . . observing.

# PART ONE

# CNN

# CHAPTER ONE
## IN THE CROSSFIRE

In the early years, I was somewhat conflicted about appearing on national TV. I had contempt for the institution and the people who ran it, and it was my job at FAIR to point out their shortcomings. But it was also my job to give FAIR a prominent public face. So I mustered my best "people skills" and tried to be friendly to all I encountered. It often felt as though I'd wandered behind enemy lines.

I made my first appearances on cable news in 1987 as a guest on CNN's *Crossfire*—the biggest and loudest nightly debate show on TV. The show had a simple format: Taking turns, a rightwing co-host would interrogate a liberal or progressive guest, and then a co-host "on the left" would interrogate a conservative guest.

I was frequently asked why I agreed to go on a show like *Crossfire*, where I was lucky to finish a sentence or two before being interrupted. I had a stock answer: First, the respectable shows weren't inviting me. Second, I knew of no other place where you could sit in a chair for 30 minutes without moving, and just from the shouting, you'd get a complete aerobic workout.

People assumed that the worst thing about *Crossfire* was the constant interruption and inability to finish your point (especially when poking holes in your opponent's argument). For me, there was something worse—receiving the annual season's greeting card signed by Patrick Buchanan, a *Crossfire* co-host.

Through incendiary writings and TV appearances, Buchanan had defined the hard right in American politics for years. He defended U.S. racial segregation and the white-supremacist apartheid system of South Africa—objecting to the idea that "white rule of a black majority is inherently wrong. . . . The Founding Fathers did not believe this." He denigrated gays as "sodomites" who were "hell bent on Satanism and suicide," and he declared that "AIDS is nature's retribution for violating the laws of nature."

Buchanan's positions often emitted more than a whiff of fascism, as when he referred to military dictators who overthrew elected governments (Gen. Franco in Spain, Gen. Pinochet in Chile) as "soldier-patriots" or praised Hitler's "courage" or questioned whether Jews had been exterminated at Treblinka.

Whenever I appeared with Buchanan, I felt this urge to belt out the song "Springtime for Hitler" from *The Producers*. I couldn't explain it. He's not the kind of guy who normally moves one to song.

In one of my first *Crossfire* confrontations with Buchanan during the beginning of Bush Sr.'s presidency, we detoured into a debate that must have resembled a new game show, *Who's the Extremist?*

Buchanan tells me he's no extremist.

BUCHANAN [shouting]: We are in the mainstream of American politics now!

COHEN: You're not in the mainstream.

BUCHANAN: You guys don't recognize that you're in a little eddy out there.

COHEN: Except you take positions defending the government of South Africa. You've spoken out for Nazi war criminals. These aren't mainstream positions.

BUCHANAN: I defended the innocence of a guy I believed was unfairly . . . [pausing, pivoting and glowering]. It does take guts, doesn't it, Mr. Cohen?

COHEN: It takes guts. It does take guts.

In the 1960s, while an editorial writer for a St. Louis daily, Buchanan was one of many journalists complicit in the FBI campaign to "neutralize" Martin Luther King Jr. Buchanan admits to publishing unverified FBI smear material on King as editorials. On a syndicated TV show in 1988, I confronted Buchanan—comparing him to "a hack writer from *Pravda* taking information from the KGB and using it in print against a Soviet dissident." I accused him of being a "state propagandist." But he was unapologetic: "All kinds of writers get information from government sources."

★ ★ ★

*Crossfire* was a pioneer in frothing TV debate, the mother of all mouthfests. But compared to what exists now on cable news (Bill O'Reilly, Sean Hannity and their imitators), *Crossfire* of the 1980s resembled the Oxford Debating Society—a 30-minute program devoted to a single *serious* topic in a two-on-two debate.*

My goal on each *Crossfire* appearance was to say something unconventional, to stretch the limits of debate—perhaps by identifying the economic interests that dominate politics and media. I went into each show hoping to make a few basic points, but even one or two points stated semi-coherently was a success amid all the crosstalk and yelling.

Sometimes it was a success just to get a wisecrack on the air. I was a *Crossfire* guest soon after the Iran-Contra scandal revealed that Reagan's White House had covertly sold high-tech weapons to America's sworn enemy, Iran's Ayatollah-led regime. Iran was then fighting a vicious war with Saddam Hussein's Iraq, which was receiving significant U.S. military aid. At the time, the hit song "We Are the World" was raising funds for famine relief in Africa. How sad, I commented, that Reagan foreign policy "could be summed up in four words: 'We *Arm* the World.'"

Another of my goals on *Crossfire* was to give free publicity to struggling, independent media outlets. Opportunity knocked when the rightwing host thought he'd come up with a terrific question: *If the mainstream media are suppressing this information, as you claim, Mr. Cohen, how do you know about it?* I took a quick gulp of air: "How do I know? *The Nation* magazine, *In These Times*, *The Progressive*, National Catholic

---

*In 2005, after adding bells and whistles and a live audience, *Crossfire* had become such an embarrassment—and more important, a ratings disappointment—that CNN terminated the show after a 22-year run. As *Crossfire* was fading, rightwinger Joe Scarborough started hosting a show at MSNBC; he says a network executive told him, "If you let someone talk for more than seven seconds on your show without interruption, then you are a failure."

*Reporter*, Pacifica Radio . . . ." As many as I could rattle off before being interrupted.

★ ★ ★

On several occasions, my debating opponent "in the crossfire" was Ben Stein, who went on to greater fame and glory as an actor and amiable Comedy Central game show host. I knew him as a hardline rightwinger, one who was tough to debate. With his flat, nasal delivery—seemingly affected, but he actually talked that way—he could make extremist sentiment sound almost sensible. And that monotone helped to obscure his often inconsistent and self-contradictory positions.

In 1987, Stein and I met on *Crossfire* to debate news coverage of extramarital activity involving then-Democratic presidential frontrunner Gary Hart. Stein declared the exposé of Hart to be "one of the highest moments of the press's utility."

> CROSSFIRE CO-HOST: How far would you have the press go? Would you say that a candidate should be asked if he's ever had a homosexual experience?

> BEN STEIN: Absolutely, as far as I'm concerned. Absolutely. Absolutely. Absolutely.

A year later, Stein and I were reunited as guests on *Crossfire*. This time reporters were pursuing an alleged relationship between GOP vice presidential candidate Dan Quayle and a female lobbyist. Give Stein credit for remaining "absolute" in his convictions. Except now that a Republican was being hounded, his convictions had rotated exactly 180 degrees.

On *Crossfire*, we weren't competing for Ben Stein's money.

> CROSSFIRE CO-HOST: Do you think the media was fair in going after Sen. Quayle on the subject of Paula Parkinson?

> BEN STEIN: Absolutely not. I think that if they started going after all the presidential

candidates on the subject of their sex lives, they could really talk about very little else. I think it's a very dangerous subject for the Democrats to open, or for anyone to open, and it's a complete irrelevancy as well.

★ ★ ★

Those first *Crossfire* appearances taught me that television is indeed a medium in which the visual trumps substance. After each guest spot, I'd call my mom for a review.

"You looked so handsome," she'd say. "I like your hair short like that."

"Mom, what did I say? Did you hear any of the points I was making?"

"And I love that tie," she'd answer.

Sometimes my friends were no more helpful: "Man, you looked like a dork in that tie. What's with the short haircut?"

## NOT SO RELIABLE SOURCES

After surviving several *Crossfire* scream-a-thons, I started appearing on more staid CNN programs, including *Larry King Live* and *Reliable Sources*, the network's show on the media. *Reliable Sources* represented a turning point for me, and not just because of the reduced decibel level. I received a stipend for some of those appearances. This was new for me—getting paid simply for yakking on TV. I was becoming a professional member of the hot-air brigade.*

I was conflicted about accepting CNN's money, roughly $200 per show. While it was FAIR's mission to promote our media criticism in the biggest media we could, it felt odd to be getting paid for it, like I was joining a club I'd long denounced.

On a *Reliable Sources* episode days after the '92 election, each panelist was asked what we disliked about election coverage. I remarked:

It's this process of always rounding up the usual pundits. They've been in the Beltway too long. They dispense conventional wis-

---

*Later, when folks would ask my daughter Cady at age 5 what her dad did for a living, she wouldn't say a word, but simply flapped her four fingers to her thumb in a jawlike motion—blah, blah, blah.

dom. And what's interesting is that Congress is now diversifying with more women, more racial minorities. I would like to see, amongst our pundit class, more leftwing pundits to balance the rightwing pundits, more women, more racial minorities. Frankly, we maybe should talk about whether there needs to be term limitations on pundits.

Such comments weren't winning me friends in the pundits union.

★ ★ ★

By 1994, Rush Limbaugh had become the dominant voice in political broadcasting—via talk radio (600 stations) and an unprecedented, 30-minute syndicated TV show devoted to his partisan monologues (200 stations). Despite his clout and close ties to the GOP leadership, most mainstream journalists had ignored Limbaugh; some, like Tim Russert and Ted Koppel, had actually praised him for getting his facts straight. Such praise evaporated in the wake of FAIR's devastating June 1994 report: *Rush Limbaugh's Reign of Error*. (This was well before Al Franken's *Big Fat Idiot* bestseller.)

FAIR exposed Limbaugh's chronic inaccuracy and debunked dozens of his claims—assertions made totally sober, years before he got hooked on pain-killing drugs.

- "There is no conclusive proof that nicotine's addictive."

- "The poorest people in America are better off than the mainstream families of Europe."

- The Clintons send their daughter to a school that requires eighth graders to write a paper on "Why I Feel Guilty Being White."

- "There are more American Indians alive today than there were when Columbus arrived."

- "There are more acres of forest land in America today than when Columbus discovered the continent in 1492." (Limbaugh was only off by a few hundred million acres.)

CNN's *Reliable Sources* invited me and rightwing media critic Brent Bozell to discuss FAIR's Limbaugh report. Limbaugh was on the advisory board of Bozell's group that purports to monitor media inaccuracy. I was asked to describe our findings:

> We looked at the issue areas that he's very concerned with, or obsessed with—the environment, economics, Clinton, Whitewater—and we found that he was concocting facts to fit his theories and his philosophy, instead of drawing his philosophy from real facts. You name it: Statements like these—"Most Canadian physicians who are themselves in need of surgery scurry across the border to get it done." Or, here's a good one on Iran-Contra. . . . "There is not one indictment; there is not one charge." Of course by that time, there were 14 indictments, and most of them led to convictions or guilty pleas.

After being grilled by panelists on Rush's errors, Bozell seemed to lose his patience for defending Limbaugh and tried to shift attention to *Reliable Sources* for not booking Limbaugh himself. Read closely.

BOZELL: Why is *he* not on this show? Why is Brent Bozell on?

HOST: In fact, I'm glad you asked that question, because we did invite him and he declined our invitation, apparently, to be here.

BOZELL: I think he's right not to lower himself to this level of having to respond to this kind of an attack from FAIR.

Bozell seemed to be channeling Martin Short's *Saturday Night Live* character Nathan Thurm, the nervous, chain-smoking prevaricator: *Oh, Rush wouldn't debate? I knew that. You think I didn't know that? He's right not to debate FAIR.*

That week, Larry King, National Public Radio and others tried to arrange debates between Limbaugh and me. He would have no part of it. "I never debate," Limbaugh had told *Talkers* magazine. "That's not what I do."

Apparently embarrassed by his performance on that show, Bozell too began refusing to debate me or anyone from FAIR. Over the years I was repeatedly invited by cable news shows to appear with him, only to be un-invited after producers granted Bozell's demand that he debate someone else—usually someone less informed and more accommodating. Howard Kurtz wrote in the *Washington Post* that "producers are going along" with Bozell's avoidance of debates. Year after year, cable news granted a leading rightwing media critic veto power over his debating foes.

★ ★ ★

Three years after the 1991 Gulf War, with U.S.-NATO air strikes looming in Bosnia, I appeared on an unusually self-critical and heated *Reliable Sources* episode. As FAIR's director, I had long blasted CNN for its overreliance on "military analysts" who were allowed to wax on without opposition or tough questions from the anchor. As if feeling guilty over this practice, CNN invited me to debate one of the network's resident experts, retired army colonel William Taylor.

Host Bernard Kalb accurately summarized our complaint about TV news: "The criticism is sharp and repeated—you bring the generals in, the colonels in, they have their contacts in the Pentagon, they're not going to go to war with their colleagues in the Pentagon, therefore you're going to get a slightly skewed, optimistic, positive view."

I explained the problem by analogy:

COHEN: You would never dream of covering the environment by bringing on expert after expert after expert who had all retired from environmental organizations after 20 or 30 years and were still loyal to those groups. You would never discuss the workplace or workers by bringing on expert after expert after expert who'd been in the labor movement and retired in good standing after 30 years. . . . When it comes to war and foreign policy, you bring on all the retired generals, retired secretaries of state.

COL. TAYLOR (irritably): What do you want, a tax auditor to come in and talk about military strategy?

COHEN: You hit it on the nail, Colonel. What you need besides the generals and the admirals who can talk about how missiles and bombs are dispatched, you need other experts. You need experts in human rights, you need medical experts, you need relief experts who know what it's like to talk about bombs falling on people.

Moments later, I seized a soundbite of a length that would have been unthinkable on *Crossfire*.

COHEN: There's this ritual, it's a familiar pattern, a routine, where mainstream journalists, after the last war or intervention, say, "Boy, we got manipulated. We were taken. But next time, we're going to be more skeptical." And then when the next time comes, it's the same reporters interviewing the same experts, who buy the distortions from the Pentagon. Those weapons in the Gulf War did not perform all that well. The Patriot was exaggerated, the success of the Patriot. The use of smart bombs was only 9 percent of the total bombs. Only 25 percent of the total bombs hit their target, and we don't hear about—the civilian casualties are usually undercounted [crosstalk]—

COL. TAYLOR (angrily): There's a real problem here. One, we won the war, the coalition, and we did it efficiently, effectively.

"We won the war . . . we did it efficiently." His triumphalism reinforced my concern that retired military brass aren't the independent analysts that viewers need to make sense of U.S. interventions.

Looking back at this 1994 CNN episode that turned a fleeting spotlight on TV's gullible war coverage, and seeing how television news reverted to form—first during Kosovo, then during the Iraq war sequel—it seems that mainstream TV journalists have misconstrued a lyric from The Who and adopted it as their motto: "We *will* be fooled again!"

## HEAD SHOTS IN THE CROSSFIRE

Unlike Limbaugh, fellow talkshow host and convicted Watergate felon G. Gordon Liddy loves to debate. He and I were guests on a surreal *Crossfire* in 1995, six days after the Oklahoma City federal building was bombed by Timothy McVeigh, an ultrarightist inflamed by gun control and the actions of federal firearms agents. Our topic was

President Clinton's comments that "reckless speech" on the airwaves and elsewhere could "push fragile people over the edge."

In the previous months, Liddy had repeatedly instructed his radio audience on how to shoot federal agents. On one show, he said, "Now if the Bureau of Alcohol, Tobacco and Firearms comes to disarm you and they are bearing arms, resist them with arms. Go for a head shot; they're going to be wearing bulletproof vests." Liddy was explicit: "They've got a big target on there, ATF. Don't shoot at that, because they've got a vest on underneath that. Head shots, head shots." "Kill the sons of bitches," he exhorted his more than a million listeners. (Days before our *Crossfire* meeting, Liddy told listeners how to build an ammonium nitrate bomb similar to McVeigh's.)

Pointing the finger at Liddy

On the *Crossfire* set, I sat next to Liddy who sat next to former Bush I chief of staff John Sununu, co-host on the right. It was even more raucous than normal, with hosts and guests shouting over each other, sometimes all four at once. Sununu asked me if I could help Clinton win a challenge from Bozell's Media Research Center, which offered to donate $100,000 to the president's favorite charity if he could name "a single credible national radio talkshow host who has advocated terrorism" against U.S. citizens or the government.

"You're sitting next to him," I told Sununu, my index finger aimed at Liddy. "Why don't you call your friends in the Media Research Center and point to him?"

Throughout the show, I tried and failed to get Sununu to criticize Liddy's radio antics. When Sununu suggested that I favored censorship, I asked if he really believed it to be censorial for radio management to tell hosts "not to advocate murdering federal agents."*

---

*Liddy made a dubious poster child for freedom of speech. He boasts that while in the Nixon White House, he had set out to assassinate columnist Jack Anderson, a Nixon critic, until higher-ups stopped him.

SUNUNU: Are there not nutcases out there that no matter what happens or what is said, they're going to do crazy things?

COHEN: Yes, there are nutcases out there, and there are nutcases on the air, and when you advocate killing federal agents by shooting them in the face, I would say you've got lunatics running the asylum.

Sununu questioned me about the "spectrum of talkshow hosts out there" and whether Clinton was "referring to Limbaugh" as one who encouraged violence.

COHEN: On many stations, it's Limbaugh, right, righter, rightest, fascist. That's your radio spectrum. On many stations, Limbaugh's almost a liberal.

SUNUNU: So you've got Limbaugh all the way over on the left?

COHEN: On many stations, he is, believe it or not.

To illustrate my point, I mentioned a Colorado Springs station that carried Limbaugh and a local talk host who advocated armed revolution and featured ultraright advocates of armed marches on Washington that would forcibly remove "traitors" from Congress. (One of the show's listeners came to Washington and sprayed nearly 30 bullets at the White House.)

I went on to distinguish Limbaugh from these extremist hosts: "Limbaugh does not advocate violence or condone it." I couldn't have been clearer.

Given my defense of Limbaugh, imagine my reaction the next day when I turned on his radio show and heard El Rushbo bellowing about the previous night's *Crossfire*: "That Jeff Cohen guy wouldn't know a fact if it hit him between the eyes."

Being accused of inaccuracy by Rush Limbaugh was like being accused of extremism by Tim McVeigh.

## "I'M NOT A LEFTIST, BUT I PLAY ONE ON TV"

For two decades, I've been preoccupied with one issue above all others: that both ends of the political spectrum get their say in the media. The issue haunted me at FAIR. It haunted my TV career. It haunts my dreams. One reason (among many) that I worked so hard to retire George W. Bush in 2004 was my nightmare that a defeated John Kerry would be hired by cable news to represent "the left" day after day on a TV debate show.

Fox News Channel often gets blamed for the standard format that pits forceful, articulate rightwingers against wimpy, halting liberals. Fox's pairing of righty heartthrob Sean Hannity with back-pedaling, barely left-of-center Alan Colmes is a prime example of this lopsided format—a mismatch depicted in an Al Franken book as *Hannity & Colmes.*

But it's wrong to blame Fox for television's center-right, GE-to-GM spectrum. That format was firmly in place years before there was a Fox News. The real culprits: CNN and PBS.

Take *Crossfire,* started by CNN in 1982 as the only nightly forum on national TV purporting to offer an ideological battle between co-hosts of left and right. *Crossfire's* co-host "on the left" for the first seven years was a haplessly ineffectual centrist, Tom Braden, a guy who makes Alan Colmes look like an ultraleft firebrand. Braden's main claim to fame was that he'd written *Eight Is Enough* and was the model for the dad character in the TV comedy series. Less well-known, and less comedic, were his years in the CIA.

In CNN's eyes, Braden apparently earned his leftist credentials by being the CIA official in charge of covert operations against the political

"Lefty" Braden and Buchanan

cal left of Western Europe. Unlike others, Braden didn't leave the spook agency as a critic or whistleblower; in 1967, after *Ramparts* exposed CIA secret funding of U.S. student groups and unions, Braden ferociously defended the agency in a column: "I'm Glad the CIA Is Immoral."

Braden was paired on *Crossfire* with ultrarightist Pat Buchanan. During the Braden-Buchanan years, LSD guru Timothy Leary referred to *Crossfire* as "the left wing of the CIA debating the right wing of the CIA." It may have been Leary's most sober observation ever.

Yippie protest leader Abbie Hoffman told me of his appearance as a guest on *Crossfire* in the 1980s. Hearing Buchanan introduced as being "on the right" and Braden "on the left," Abbie said he refused to play along with the sham and caused a minor disruption by asking to have himself seated on the left—"with Braden in the center, where he belonged."

I guested several times on *Crossfire* with the tired 70-something as my alleged ally. Once as I took my seat on the set, seeing Braden totally caked up with makeup, my first impulse was to reach over to take a pulse. My second impulse: flee the studio.

In a 1988 *Crossfire* appearance, when I criticized the conservative tilt of TV punditry and debates restricted to right versus center, Buchanan could mount only a feeble defense of Braden: "What do you think is sitting next to me? What do you think this is, a potted plant?"

"A healthy Ficus," observed a *Mother Jones* writer, "would add more balance."

The taboo against genuine progressives as hosts was even clearer when *Crossfire* needed substitutes "on the left" and CNN chose Beltway centrists like Jodie Powell (President Carter's press secretary) and Morton Kondracke (yes, the guy now on Fox . . . and no, he was no more progressive then). These were men who would never declare themselves to be "on the left" in real life; they seemed to wince when CNN made them say it on television.

For Braden and many of his successors, being "on the left" was less a self-description to be proud of than an accusation to deny. Seeing liberals on TV backpedal night after night in the face of the Buchanans and Hannitys helps create a public image of the American Left as weak, evasive, lacking in values—and the American Right as clear, firm and moral. Pundit TV has defined not only a skewed spectrum of debate but a road map for defeat of liberal politicians. Ask Gore and Kerry.

Years before Fox was invented, FAIR ran full-page ads spotlighting TV's "left" pundits.

★ ★ ★

On both CNN and PBS, one of TV's longest-running stand-ins for the left has been Mark Shields, even while his promo materials denied any ideological leanings: "Mark Shields is free of any political tilt." When John Roberts became our country's chief justice, Shields wrote a scalding attack . . . not on the rightwing judge (whom he actually praised) but on a feminist leader who opposed Roberts. Shields is a smart, articulate guy—but he's no more an advocate for the American Left than Mel Gibson is an advocate for reform Judaism.

## GHOST OF JOE MCCARTHY

As FAIR's director in the 1980s and '90s, I had the opportunity to "dialogue with" (more accurately "bitch at") dozens of TV news executives and decision-makers about their choices—including the matter of who would represent the left and right on debate shows.

Why were TV's rightists chosen from the banks of the Bavarian Danube while "leftists" came from the ranks of the CIA (Braden) or the *Wall Street Journal* (CNN's Al Hunt)? Why were TV rightists invited to address throngs of activists at conservative gatherings, but TV leftists wouldn't be caught dead at a labor rally or antiwar protest unless their limousines got stuck on the wrong street? And wasn't the systematic exclusion of genuine progressive advocates a form of censorship?

It became clear to me that the exclusion was partly a legacy of McCarthyism—a fear of the left, and of associating with the left. Television was born in the era of Joe McCarthy, red-baiting and the blacklists. TV execs were not timid about hiring a hard-right America-Firster like Buchanan. But what would happen to the Suit who gave prominent slots to unabashed leftists, the kind of folks routinely demonized as "un-American"?

In 1990, I met with decision-makers at ABC's *Nightline* after FAIR's 40-month survey of the program revealed a stark bias in favor of conservative guests, including far-right ones. Topping Ted Koppel's white-male-dominated guest list were former secretaries of state Henry Kissinger and Al Haig, former assistant secretary of state Elliott Abrams (best remembered for lying to Congress about Iran-Contra) and Rev. Jerry Falwell, who offered his expertise about AIDS on one show and homosexuality on another.

When I asked why *Nightline* never invited credible experts such as Daniel Ellsberg—the Vietnam-era Pentagon planner who became a whistle-blower and peace advocate—I learned that the boss saw him as an "extremist." Given that Falwell, Abrams and Pat Buchanan recently had 31 *Nightline* appearances between them, I expressed my disbelief that "extremism" would disqualify anyone.*

Years later, when I worked at MSNBC, I was told that former Attorney General Ramsey Clark was on some sort of blacklist and wasn't supposed to be invited on the air.

★ ★ ★

There was another factor causing leftist pundits to be shunned in favor of tepid liberals: sponsorship. More precisely: the fear of sponsor flight. TV executives may not be sophisticated in their knowledge of the political left, but they know that bona fide progressives tend to criticize large corporations—a historical truth from Martin Luther King Jr. and Walter Reuther to Ralph Nader and Michael Moore. And large corporations sponsor all the pundit shows. For years, two conservative, politically active firms sponsored most of these shows: General Electric and Archer Daniels Midland.

Given TV's unwillingness to spook sponsors, it's no wonder that CNN turns to corporate-friendly liberals from the CIA and *Wall Street Journal*.

★ ★ ★

Whatever the causes, TV's truncated center-right pairings have an impact on national discourse—helping to push the fulcrum of debate farther and farther rightward.

---

*After FAIR's *Nightline* study was released, a black columnist dubbed the program "Whiteline." A Pennsylvania daily accompanied its report on the study with a photo of Koppel seated next to Kermit the Frog, who appeared on *Nightline* once to explain economic terms; the caption called it a "a rare public appearance with a minority group member."

# CNN'S MR. UNRELIABLE

In 1989, CNN announced that Tom Braden was leaving *Crossfire*, vacating the only seat on national TV explicitly reserved for someone "on the left." The opening sparked intense activism by FAIR and allies urging CNN to end its charade and hire a genuine progressive. It was an unprecedented mobilization—as members of the public and organized constituencies asserted their right to have a say in who represented them on TV.

In my discussions with CNN executives at the time—and with other Suits in the years to come—I argued that in view of the serious problems facing our country, it's not only good journalism but good for democracy to hear solutions from a broad spectrum of views.

And I maintained that real debates would boost their ratings and profits. That a large unserved audience of progressives was hungering for representation on TV and would support a show that gave them voice. But the ghost of Joe McCarthy seemed to scare away the hidden hand of Adam Smith.

The battle for *Crossfire*'s left seat came down to a two-man race: *New Republic* editor Michael Kinsley vs. activist-author Mark Green. Both had experience subbing for Braden.

Kinsley was an informed and clever writer. But on TV he had a nerdy, Steve Urkel–like presence and seemed more interested in demonstrating his cleverness than persuading viewers toward the left. Although Kinsley was more glib and alert than Braden (who wasn't?), he was no more bona fide a progressive advocate. A sympathetic profile in *New York* magazine a few years earlier had observed that Kinsley's "longest needles are reserved for the left."

Shortly before the *Crossfire* job opened, Kinsley had praised right-wing British prime minister Margaret Thatcher in a *Time* column headlined "Thatcher for President?"—perhaps the world's only "leftist" to laud her. In a *Washington Post* column near the end of apartheid, "Rights for Whites," Kinsley sided with South Africa's last white prime minister against Nelson Mandela on the way forward for that country.

Progressive leaders (and *Crossfire* producers) preferred Green, a Democratic activist and author of books critical of corporate power. In a tally of left-of-center Americans or leaders, Green would have outpolled Kinsley 95 to 5.

But unlike many decisions in TV, CNN's choice didn't hinge on audience, polls or focus groups. CNN hired Kinsley.

Apparently, the wishes of one rightwinger outweighed the entire American Left: *Crossfire* co-host Pat Buchanan. According to the *Washington Times*, a rightwing paper close to Buchanan, he played a big role in choosing his debating partner: "CNN sources said Mr. Green was rejected because of Mr. Buchanan's personal contempt for him, and because he probably would try to use the position as a mouth-to-mouth resuscitator for his seemingly deceased political career." (Ironically, Buchanan would soon use *Crossfire* as a platform for his own much loftier political ambitions.)

So the left had its new, not-so-telegenic TV spokesmodel. Under editor Kinsley (and owner Marty Peretz), the *New Republic* supported the Contra war against Nicaragua and other Reaganite hard-right foreign policy adventures in the 1980s. Selecting the *New Republic*'s top editor to represent the left might have made sense in 1939 when it was a leading progressive journal; by 1989, it provided yet more evidence that actual progressives need not apply for nightly duty on national TV . . . and that imposters were needed. Call it "journalistic blackface."

Two days after Kinsley's hiring, *Los Angeles Times* TV critic Howard Rosenberg called on *Crossfire* to "get the labeling right: Pat Buchanan from the far right and Michael Kinsley from slightly left of center."

In that day's *New York Daily News*, Kinsley described himself as "unreliably left"—prompting suggestions that he excuse himself from the program on those nights he felt particularly "unreliable." I would later learn that his unreliability caused problems for *Crossfire*'s producers.

★ ★ ★

My guest appearances on *Crossfire* continued after Kinsley became co-host. He was usually supposed to be my teammate in the two-on-two tag-team debates. But like Braden, Kinsley often provided little help— a complaint I heard for years from feminist and civil rights leaders (several of whom shied away from the show for that reason).

Once I appeared as a *Crossfire* guest to debate whether news media had gone tabloid in covering events such as the federal assault on the Koresh cult compound in Waco, Texas. I offered the traditional progressive (and hardly controversial) view that TV news exploited certain stories for ratings and profit. But since Kinsley was inclined to defend corporate media and TV news, he was teamed with a spokesperson for the News Directors Association. I was supposed to be on the team of rightwing co-host John Sununu, who has contempt for journalism and said virtually nothing I could agree with.

When it was suggested that I wanted news outlets to behave as public charities, I took a nuanced position: "Earning a profit is not the sin. It's doing unethical reporting. It's grabbing people on sensational stories just to pump your own ratings."

But moments later, a perturbed Kinsley was diagnosing my problem: "Your problem seems to be with capitalism."

It was not uncommon for me to be red-baited on national TV—that happened regularly when conservatives sought to shift the discussion from my arguments to my alleged extremism. It felt quite strange to be red-baited by the host "on the left."*

★   ★   ★

Kinsley's defense of corporate media practices was not unusual for TV liberals. In debates on whether media firms put profits ahead of ethics—for example, Hollywood's mindless violence—it's commonly the Buchanans and Hannitys who wax righteously indignant about media ethics, while TV "leftists" come off as apologists for immoral, indefensible practices.

———

*On CNN three months after my Kinsley run-in, I encountered more generic red-baiting from a rightwing editor who lacked factual argumentation: Emmett Tyrrell. Debating whether mainstream media tilt right or left, he asked, "Are you from Yugoslavia or someplace?"

COHEN: When you analyze an institution, you begin with who owns it.

TYRRELL: You must be the last Marxist on Earth.

COHEN: And then you look at the spectrum of who gets to comment.

TYRRELL: If you're a Marxist—

COHEN: On this network, you have a spectrum on some shows, for example, that goes from the right wing, like Mona Charen and [Bob] Novak, to the left wing, which is Al Hunt of the *Wall Street Journal*. Now you probably believe that the *Wall Street Journal* is a leftwing institution.

TYRRELL: No, I don't.

I once declined an invitation to join a *Hannity & Colmes* debate on Hooters, the restaurant chain where waitresses serve as appetizers. I did watch the discussion. What I remember is left co-host Colmes seeming to apologize for Hooters, while rightist Hannity railed against the exploitation of women workers.

Years of such debates may have sent a skewed message to many Americans that the left has no moral foundation.

## YOU CAN'T FLY A PLANE WITH JUST A RIGHT WING

Neither a plane nor a political system will be stable if the pull is only in one direction. On TV, "leftists" are typically moderate Democrats who rally around the party brass, including when President Clinton was borrowing Republican policies to govern from the supposed center. By contrast, TV rightists are rarely willing to defend waffling or moderation by their party leadership or president. Even as GOP leaders moved further and further right in recent years, CNN's Pat Buchanan and Bob Novak echoed movement conservatives in continually goading their party to become still more extreme.

Buchanan's criticisms of the first Bush administration became so intense that he left *Crossfire* in 1991 to challenge Bush Sr. for the Republican nomination. At the 1992 GOP convention, Buchanan declared "culture war" on gays, feminists and liberals in a speech that, according to columnist Molly Ivins, "sounded better in the original German."

Soon after conceding defeat, Buchanan returned to *Crossfire* to regain his visible perch in front of nearly a million Americans each night, the envy of other presidential candidates.

Buchanan exited *Crossfire* again in 1995 to run for president again—with CNN's revolving door spinning like Macy's during a pre-Christmas sale. On Buchanan's last show before hitting the campaign trail, an obliging Kinsley helped Buchanan hold

Kinsley lends a hand.

up a sign with the 1-800-GO-PAT-GO number that viewers could call to donate to Buchanan's campaign. The moment epitomized the submissive role played by TV's lukewarm liberals for their rightwing co-stars.

Four years earlier, when Jerry Brown insisted on mentioning his 800 number on *Crossfire* during his insurgent campaign for the Democratic presidential nomination, CNN told Brown not to show up at the studio. In Brown's absence that night, all four *Crossfire* pundits, from right to "left," ridiculed him: "Isn't Jerry Brown making a complete joke of himself," asked Kinsley, "carrying on like this?"

★ ★ ★

Imagine if the American Right had been represented year after year on TV not by the Buchanans and Hannitys, but by moderate Republican pundits allied with Christine Todd Whitman and Arlen Spector—moderates dismissive of their party's activists.

Now imagine that the American Left had been represented on TV not by the Kinsleys and Colmeses, but by progressive pundits like Barbara Ehrenreich and Jim Hightower.

Neither scenario is easy to imagine—which says a lot about the real bias of TV news.

★ ★ ★

One of the oddities of CNN was its founder Ted Turner, good-ole-boy maverick, quirky entrepreneur and "mouth of the South." When he launched CNN, Turner was quoted as saying that a "bunch of pinkos" ran ABC, CBS and NBC. In 1985, he joined forces with a rightwing effort led by arch-conservative Sen. Jesse Helms to take over CBS because of its supposed "liberal bias." But rightists soon saw Turner himself as a symbol of "The Liberal Media" after he spoke out for the environment and arms talks with the Soviets.

No matter what Turner said in speeches about pollution or nuclear arms, CNN's content was unaffected—persisting in its center-right Kinsley-to-Buchanan spectrum. Year after year, advocates of corporate power and war had a platform on CNN that green and peace voices lacked. FAIR was never able to reach Turner; he rebuffed well-documented, progressive criticism of CNN's biases. By 1996, Turner's influence at CNN diminished after he sold the network and Turner Broadcasting to Time Warner for about $8 billion.

The Time Warner–Turner merger was first proposed as President Clinton and a Republican Congress were promoting their Telecommunications "Reform" Act, drafted by fat media companies to allow them to grow still fatter. Consumer advocates dubbed it the "Time Warner Enrichment Act." With CNN and other big news outlets barely covering the most important media legislation in 60 years, a consumer group tried to buy time on CNN for ads denouncing the bill. CNN refused to sell time. Clinton signed the bill in February 1996. Soon after, the feds approved Time Warner's takeover of Turner and CNN.

In 2004, Ted Turner published a powerful essay in the *Washington Monthly* (he says major dailies had rejected it) attacking corporate media censorship and conglomerates like Time Warner. He called for new federal "rules that will break these huge companies to pieces."

★ ★ ★

Well after Turner had been pushed aside, veteran *Time* magazine editor Walter Isaacson became CNN's chair in 2001 and immediately created a spectacle by traipsing to Capitol Hill for private meetings with GOP leaders over complaints that CNN was unfair to conservatives. "I wanted to hear their concerns," said Isaacson. A top Republican staffer quoted Isaacson as saying he wanted to change CNN's culture: "Give us guidance on how to attract conservatives." It was a powerful show of obeisance.

Genuflecting to the right was the natural bent of every cable news executive I ever met.

# CHAPTER TWO
## STAR SEARCH

In November 1995, Michael Kinsley announced he was leaving *Crossfire*. FAIR had waited for that day like believers await the Rapture. Kinsley didn't rise up to the Kingdom of Heaven but to the Kingdom of Microsoft, to be founding editor of its online magazine *Slate*.

As he was exiting *Crossfire*, after having identified himself as "on the left" night after night for six years, Kinsley was asked about his politics by reporter Howard Kurtz. Kinsley called himself "a wishy-washy moderate."

Give the guy credit for honesty, even if a few years too late.

Kinsley's departure sparked a free-for-all at *Crossfire*, which was among CNN's top two shows in audience size. FAIR and other progressive groups contacted the network to urge an authentic spokesperson this time, while CNN executives were swarmed by pseudo-left Beltway pundits, their friends and agents.

CNN's search for a replacement got off to a strange (but familiar) start when the first person tested for the job was Margaret Carlson. She was a *Time* magazine writer who'd complained on CNN two years earlier that then-mayoral candidate Rudy Giuliani would not be the "union-busting tough guy who's going to come in and clean up New York." Leftists for union-busting?

During her two nights of tryouts, Carlson couldn't bring herself to use the traditional sign-off at the end of the show. Instead of "From the left, I'm Margaret Carlson," she ended with "From Washington, I'm Margaret Carlson." It was a rare bit of truth in advertising—but it clearly confused co-host Bob Novak.

The oddball sign-off prompted TV critic Howard Rosenberg to quip, "No, no, no. The show is supposed to be balanced, not the co-hosts." Rosenberg's column urged CNN to end the phony clash

"between a militant far-right-winger and a brutally fanatical centrist."
He argued that *Crossfire* would be true to its billing only if "the cable
channel does the right thing and picks a true advocate from the left."

★ ★ ★

Two weeks after Carlson's tryout, I received the shock of my life when
*Crossfire*'s top executive called. He told me that he'd recently seen me
on Phil Donahue's daytime show, blasting CNN and others for censor-
ing progressive voices, as Phil held up a poster-size blowup of FAIR's
"I'm Not a Leftist, but I Play One on TV" ad—featuring a photo of
Kinsley.

But the CNN exec wasn't calling to complain about my criticism of
*Crossfire*. He was calling to see if I would suit up for an on-air screen test
for the co-host job. He told me there'd be a dozen other candidates.

I said yes without hesitation, while wondering if I was little more
than leftwing window-dressing for CNN's star search. No matter, I
was determined to give it my all.

If *Crossfire* hired me to replace Kinsley, it would have marked the
most abrupt switch from foes to allies since the Hitler-Stalin pact. Not
easy to imagine. Yet it was hard to suppress daydreams of wealth and
fame and TV's premier platform for advocacy. And what a victory for
FAIR and its allies, if they could push CNN into finally hiring a genuine progressive.

I wanted to believe the invite
was due to the strength of my
guest appearances on CNN over
the years. But it may have had
more to do with a historic grassroots upsurge that included an
"Open Letter to CNN" signed by
15 groups (including Sierra Club,
Greenpeace, Rainbow Coalition,
National Council of La Raza, National Organization for Women
and unions such as the NEA and
Steelworkers) representing "millions of mainstream Americans,
and some of the leading progressive constituencies in our country."

The letter urged CNN to "choose a bona fide advocate for progressive causes and activism—and not a middle-of-the-road establishment

pundit or political figure who just happens to be a Democrat." It complained of *Crossfire*'s history of "imbalanced, incomplete and sometimes fuzzy debate."

The best narrative on what ensued comes from populist commentator Jim Hightower in his classic 1997 book *There's Nothing in the Middle of the Road but Yellow Stripes and Dead Armadillos*. (Jim did for book titles what James Joyce did for sentences.) Referring to *Crossfire* as "verbal mud wrestling for news junkies," Hightower said that pitting Kinsley against the Buchanans and Novaks was "like sending Tweety Bird into a cockfight." But there was good news:

> Mercifully, Kinsley resigned the "left's" chair in 1996 to accept a sinecure at Microsoft, putting his "liberalism" in the employ of one of America's leading monopolists. At last, though, this meant there was a chance to put someone in that seat who has real teeth to bare. *Crossfire*'s producers led progressive activists to believe that they were serious about wanting a contender, a true progressive scrapper to join the show, so names were submitted. A number of us pushed hard for Jeff Cohen.

Modesty (and copyright limits) compel me to stop Hightower's excerpt here. Suffice it to say that he went on to describe me as "smart, scrappy, knowledgeable, experienced, articulate and an unabashed progressive."

Fairness compels me to add what Hightower wrote immediately thereafter: "Plus, he met a key criterion for the job: He was willing to do it, willing to spend a significant portion of his life in televised shouting matches with the likes of Novak and Sununu. Such is the price of show biz."

## NOVAK VS. COHEN

"On the left, Jeff Cohen!"

I never expected to hear those words. It felt thrilling yet totally incongruous. "Hey, I'm actually *on* the left—what am I doing in Kinsley's chair?" But there I was.

On my first night as *Crossfire* co-host, I was cordially and accurately introduced by fellow co-host Bob Novak as "a longtime advocate of making sure the voice of the real left is heard."

The topic was standard for that era, January 1996: Hillary Clinton and the investigations swirling around her and her husband stemming from years-old financial dealings in Arkansas, including a real estate deal called Whitewater. So I was supposed to be playing defense. But as a host, it was easy to take the offensive. The issue wasn't Hillary's corruption, I maintained; she was the victim of sexist fear and resentment.

My opening question to the conservative guest was a run-on (but concise compared to a typical Charlie Rose question):

Wouldn't you agree with me that much of the venom being aimed at Hillary Clinton—and I've been monitoring rightwing talk shows and televangelists since 1992, before Whitewater was much talked about as an issue—doesn't much of the venom stem from the simple fact that Hillary Clinton is a strong career woman, and antifeminist rightwing forces in the Republican Party simply detest her for it?

Me and Novak

Wow. This was fun. You couldn't get away such long-windedness as a mere guest. But I was carrying the football, sprinting downfield, no tackler in sight.

I expounded on my first question by bringing up GOP Hillary-bashing and the 1992 Republican convention: "I saw speaker after speaker get up there—and this is before Whitewater was much talked about. . . . Speaker after speaker denounced her as a 'radical feminist.' She's 'antifamily.' Roger Ailes, the Republican strategist, made fun of her—that she looked so silly in an apron."*

The show was a breeze.

---

*From the convention podium, Pat Buchanan had denounced Hillary as a "radical feminist." GOP national chair Rich Bond called her "antifamily" just before the convention. Ailes' full quote was vintage: "Hillary Clinton in an apron is like Michael Dukakis in a tank."

★ ★ ★

The next morning, a *Crossfire* producer called me at my elegant D.C. hotel room provided by CNN. She said I'd turned in a strong performance—and she needed to talk over possible topics for that evening, one possibility being capital punishment. She said she was sure I'd have a strong anti–death penalty position. Producers told me that their job was much easier working with a co-host who was reliably left each and every night. With Kinsley, some topics apparently had to be avoided.

The death penalty was a perfect issue for me. That night I co-hosted again with Novak. Our two guests "in the crossfire" were Sister Helen Prejean, who wrote the book *Dead Man Walking* (which Susan Sarandon, Sean Penn and Tim Robbins turned into a riveting movie), and George Pataki, who rode the issue of reinstating the death penalty into New York's governor's mansion a year earlier, evicting Mario Cuomo.

Confronting Pataki on his signature issue gave me a close-up look at pure ambition and opportunism. Criminologists can't find evidence that capital punishment deters crime. Pataki insists on it. Dozens of innocents, including an African American high school basketball teammate of Pataki's, have been wrongly convicted of the capital crime of murder. Pataki insists his death penalty law is foolproof.

When Pataki argued that the death penalty would deter a hold-up artist from killing a cop (though FBI statistics show cop-killings are much more frequent in states *with* capital punishment), Sister Helen was not charitable toward Pataki: "He's staking his career on executing some people and basing it on this bogus stuff that it might deter somebody who's thinking about killing."

I asked Pataki a closing question aimed at getting us out of the muck of wrestling over deterrence and FBI stats:

Debating Gov. Pataki

> COHEN: I just want to ask the governor one final question. Virtually every democratic Western country has abolished the death

penalty. We're going in the opposite direction with more executions. We're following the example of Iran, China, Saudi Arabia—these are countries with death penalties. Why aren't we following the example of the civilized Western democratic countries instead of these totalitarian countries?

GOV. PATAKI: And the State of Israel has the death penalty as well.

A deft and slippery response to invoke a country that reserves the death penalty solely for Nazi war criminals.

After thanking and excusing the guests, each *Crossfire* episode concluded with a short back-and-forth segment between the co-hosts—called, revealingly enough, the Yip Yap. This one ended as follows:

NOVAK: Jeff, you know, I don't know whether capital punishment is a deterrent. I don't much care. What it is—it provides vengeance against some of these brutal killers, and maybe countries that don't provide that vengeance are just overcivilized.

COHEN: But, Bob, you're sounding like the Ayatollahs of Iran. I think the death penalty is *not* a deterrent. It wastes money because it costs more money to execute than life imprisonment. It's racist.

NOVAK: Vengeance.

COHEN: It's immoral.

NOVAK: Do you deny vengeance?

COHEN: Yes. I'm not for vengeance. From the left, I'm Jeff Cohen. Good night for *Crossfire*.

NOVAK. From the right, for vengeance, I'm Robert Novak. Join us again next time for another edition of *Crossfire*.

I'm well aware that only a minority of Americans, albeit a growing minority, join me in opposing capital punishment. But I'll bet that many death penalty supporters among CNN's million viewers that night had second thoughts—seeing the pundit on their side reduce the whole issue to the need for vengeance.

Decades ago, Novak acquired the nickname "The Prince of Darkness" from colleagues in elite media circles, a label he seemed to relish.

In 2003, he would gain more infamy by outing an undercover CIA officer, part of a White House effort to punish a critic of Bush's Iraq war. But I must confess that I enjoyed working with him, largely because his extremism made it easy for me to come off as reasoned and commonsensical.

★ ★ ★

During one of my co-hosting appearances, I was breezing along confidently, thinking "Gee, I'm made for this job!" Until I hit a speed bump. The producer had instructed us preshow that, to ensure equal time, Novak and I had to follow her directions transmitted to us via earpieces. But as we headed to a commercial break, with the producer repeatedly telling my co-host to toss to me, he just kept on talking. Annoyed, I asked during the break, "Bob, didn't you hear the producer?"

He smiled at me, the rookie, and muttered something about "running out the clock."

## IN THE FINALS

My initial tryouts went very well. The show's producers thought so. So did TV critics. And *Crossfire* started hearing from many dozens of viewers and progressive leaders by phone, mail, even emails (Internet activism was new then), urging that I be hired. A CNN exec told me no other candidate sparked significant grassroots support.

The only off-key note came from my FAIR colleagues, dismayed by my zealous defense of Hillary Clinton, a centrist figure not beloved at FAIR. When I returned to work, I found a placard with my picture posted on the office bulletin board—inverting FAIR's famous slogan to take a jab at me: "I'm Not a Centrist, but I Play One on TV."

Most of those tested for the *Crossfire* job received just two days of tryouts. So when I was invited back to co-host three more shows, I had made it into the finals. Of the more than a dozen originally tested, only five others got callbacks.

Still, I forced myself to be realistic about my chances. This was, after all, the network that had felt comfortable with Braden, Kinsley and even Kondracke in that seat. I calculated the odds of CNN hiring me as slightly better than the odds of Christian Broadcasting hiring Madonna.

FAIR had long noted that genuine left advocates are critics of corporate greed and irresponsibility—and that such views are not welcome in a media system run by conglomerates for whom greed is a *raison d'être*. Most of my competitors for the position were safe: Beltway insiders, corporate lobbyists or fundraisers from big business.

I was not so safe. CNN was worried about sponsor reactions to a genuinely left host, and that was made clear to me. As co-host, I did something rare on *Crossfire* by denouncing the political influence of specific firms, such as agribusiness giant Archer Daniels Midland. There was a concern I might go out of my way to attack *Crossfire*'s sponsors. I tried to assure CNN that while I would never yield on my skepticism of corporate power and would criticize corporations when appropriate to the topic, I was not ideologically compelled to trash our sponsors.

And who was *Crossfire*'s main sponsor? A company I had long criticized, General Electric, with interests in war, nuclear power, regulation, trade and a dozen other areas. I knew and they knew that, often enough, criticism of GE *would* be appropriate to the topic.

None of these concerns attached to another *Crossfire* finalist, Bob Beckel, a middle-of-the-road Democratic operative and corporate lobbyist who had long co-hosted CNN's *Crossfire Sunday* "from the left." Near the end of the tryouts for Kinsley's job, the *Washington Post* exposed Beckel's recent participation in a private strategy session convened by the American Petroleum Institute on how the oil industry could better promote its efforts to undermine environmental laws.

It was no big deal to CNN. Beckel represented the "left" that night on *Crossfire*.

## AIR SUNUNU

On my next two *Crossfire* episodes, my co-host was John Sununu, a former New Hampshire governor who became White House chief of staff for Bush Sr. He was known for arrogance: shouting down Cabinet officials, hanging up on Congress members.

Though a "fiscal conservative," Sununu caused a scandal by using military aircraft to fly to ski trips in Colorado, dental appointments in Boston and visits with his parents in Florida. At the height of the "Air Sununu" controversy—with his wings clipped and restrictions imposed on his fights—he had a taxpayer-financed chauffer-driven limo transport him from the White House to a rare stamp auction in New York City. The Bush emissary who broke the news to Sununu that it was time for him to resign was none other than "first son" George W. Bush.

Sununu and I had the kind of chemistry not seen on TV since Bill Buckley and Gore Vidal squared off—and almost came to blows—during the riotous 1968 Democratic convention in Chicago. Our clashes had pique, passion and more crosstalk than a 1930s party-line phone. I hadn't experienced such condescension since graduating from kindergarten. On one show, he called me "preposterous"; on another,

If you knew Sununu . . .

he said, "You live in fantasy land" and "You're talking in circles."

My first show co-hosting with Sununu was a brawl over campaign finance. The guests were progressive Sen. Russ Feingold and conservative Sen. Mitch McConnell, who argued that there was *too little* private money in U.S. politics. I asked McConnell to comment on Western European elections, which have much bigger voter turnouts and little private money. Before I could get an answer, Sununu roared, "That's the dumbest thing I've ever heard."

I moved the discussion to our country's "pay-for-play system" by asking McConnell about his Senate ally Bob Dole, soon to be the GOP presidential candidate:

> Sen. Dole has received over a million dollars from the Ernest & Julio Gallo winemakers over the years to his various committees, and Sen. Dole was instrumental in passing a measure that saved Gallo tens of millions of dollars in estate taxes. Isn't it that kind of relationship—that politician coziness with big moneyed interests— that turns off Americans?

McConnell simply changed the subject and didn't answer. Later, I took another crack at the same subject:

> COHEN: Sen. McConnell, whenever I see big corporate money flooding into Washington—whether it was in support of

NAFTA, whether it was to kill healthcare reform, whether it's in support of the telecommunication bill, which is good for a number of corporate interests—it seems that the side that's flooding Washington with money is the side that wins. It's almost like those who write the checks write the laws. Can you give me three recent examples where the side that didn't have the money—perhaps it's the side that supported middle-class interests—where they won?

SEN. McCONNELL: It happens all the time

Yet he didn't offer a single example.

★  ★  ★

The next night's show was focused on anti-Washington "outsider" candidates for president; magazine heir and GOP challenger Steve Forbes was gaining on Dole thanks to a self-financed ad barrage. I sought to provoke my conservative guest, a Republican strategist, by invoking a more authentic outsider candidate:

I think you can judge the bonafidedness of an outsider by how the establishment press relates to them. I remember when Jerry Brown ran in 1992—in the so-called objective articles in *Newsweek* and *Time*, he was "fringe," he was "unfit," he was "the mad monk," he was "the character assassin." How would you compare the coverage of someone who I think was a more bona fide outsider, Jerry Brown, representing the majority of the people, working-class people, and how the media is covering Forbes?

Before the guest could answer, a miffed Sununu jumped in to offer his response about Brown: "An eccentric is equivalent to a representative of the people?"

Dismissing someone as "eccentric" is not unusual on pundit shows. It did sound off-key that night, given that our other guest was . . . Jerry Brown.

Sununu's essence emerged when I made an attempt at small talk during a break: "Hey, John, what about you for president?" His response: "No, I had that job already."

A humble reference to his time as leader of the Free World.

# ON THE LEFT, A FEMININE WEENIE

For my fifth and final tryout, I was relieved to be co-hosting with Novak again. The topic was "The Future of Feminism"—a huge feminist expo was occurring in D.C. that weekend. One of our guests was National Organization for Women president Patricia Ireland, a strong debater who'd been leery of *Crossfire* partly because of the weakness of co-hosts "on the left." But she was happy to appear with me and show support by appearing.

The other guest was Christina Hoff Sommers, a shrill critic of the feminist leadership and newfound hero of the right wing. She had built a career by declaring herself a feminist bold enough to denounce feminist leaders as bitter, man-hating extremists.

My opening question went after her central claim:

Professor Hoff Sommers, when you look at the gains that the feminist movement has made in recent years—more job opportunities; more equal pay for equal work; you don't get fired if you're a woman worker and you get pregnant; graduate school has opened up; reproductive freedom; there's this national network of battered women's shelters and women's health centers that feminists have started. Don't you sometimes feel silly, sort of off on the sidelines, calling the mainstream feminist groups and leaders who've accomplished so much—calling them extremists? And isn't that what the suffragettes were called when they demanded a woman's right to vote?

Hoff Sommers' response: It's because of women's gains that today's feminists seem "caught in a time warp." She attacked the feminist expo: "The rage is there. They're reviling men. . . . It's angry. It's bitter."

I pointed out that NOW has male members—and that I'd never detected any man-hating in 20 years of reading NOW's literature.

Patricia and I raise feminist consciousness.

In no time, Novak was squaring off with Patricia Ireland in predictable ways:

NOVAK: I just want to stay on this sexual thing for one moment. Do you think it's unfair to say that the feminist movement today, that the movement that Christina really criticizes, has a strong lesbian content to it?

IRELAND: Oh, I think that it is a key issue, just like eliminating racism is. If we don't provide equal opportunity and civil rights for everyone, I think that we are going to lose the idealism that propels this movement forward.

NOVAK: Let me ask you, frankly, as a reporter: Are many of the people at the [Feminist] Expo '96 conference lesbians?

IRELAND: Well, we don't take names.

Later in the show, I asked the professor about her feminist credentials (not often probed in previous interviews): "Professor Hoff Sommers, you say you're a feminist. I don't know of any other feminist whose work has been repeatedly praised by perhaps the loudest voice of antifeminism and Republicanism in our country, Rush Limbaugh." And I asked about her book attacking feminist leaders: "The book was funded by Olin, Bradley and Carthage, which are three rightwing, antifeminist foundations. How do you explain it?"

"Patricia Ireland wouldn't give me a grant," Hoff Sommers responded. "The National Organization for Women would not give me a grant."

The pairing of Ireland and Hoff Sommers was typical of TV debates on issues about women or African Americans: A leader of a civil rights group with many thousands of members is paired with a think-tank-funded conservative critic with little mass following. What was unusual about this show is that the critic's credentials and funding had been questioned.

For all her talk about how feminist leaders are bitter and angry, it was Hoff Sommers who departed the *Crossfire* set furious; she didn't leave until being told a couple times that her portion of the show had ended. As Ireland exited, she was beaming, almost angelic.

The yip-yap segment opened with Novak asking me if I thought "it would be better if men were a little feminized, became more feministic."

I responded that it would in fact be good if men "became more feminist." Then he corrected me:

NOVAK: Feminine! Feminine, I said.

COHEN: No. I'm saying "feminist."

NOVAK: Well, what's the difference?

COHEN: The difference is feminist means you're a man who supports independent women and equality for women.

NOVAK: Kind of weenie and weak-kneed and—

COHEN: Nothing weenie—

NOVAK: Want the government to take care of them.

COHEN: Nothing weenie about supporting strong women.

NOVAK: Can't stand up for themselves.

COHEN: What I think is weenie is the men who are afraid of strong women.

NOVAK: How about the women like my wife who are pro-life, believe in raising a family and are appalled by these conventions of the shrieking females?

COHEN: Feminists believe in raising a family. I've got a 4-year-old daughter, and I thank Patricia Ireland and Ellie Smeal and the feminist movement for opening all these doors for my daughter. From the left, I'm Jeff Cohen.

It was my best performance as co-host. But was it too good?

★　★　★

Four days later, Novak and I appeared at Iowa State University in a not-for-TV debate on media bias. I opened with a mock apology to CNN for FAIR's criticism that programs like *Crossfire* didn't offer pundits anywhere as far left as Novak is far right: "After working with Bob, I see CNN's predicament—how do you find anyone as far left as Bob is far right? Especially since Chairman Mao is dead." The crowd roared with laughter, and I even detected a smile from Novak.

During a commercial break on *Crossfire*, I had asked Novak, "Who's further right, you or Buchanan?" No contest, he said, since Buchanan was taking liberal, New Deal positions on economics: "I was an Eisenhower Republican in the '50s," said Novak, "and I've moved further right every year since." It was unthinkable that a TV "leftist" would ever say "I was a JFK Democrat in the '60s and have moved further left ever since."

## AND THE WINNER IS . . .

After my final tryouts, even more calls and letters poured into CNN on my behalf from activists, members of Congress, union leaders and prominent individuals like Bill Moyers, Phil Donahue, Jesse Jackson and Ralph Nader.

Some urged my hiring because I was a "movement progressive," the kind of advocate they invite to their rallies and activist conferences, a counterweight to a Pat Buchanan—not just a moderate Democratic consultant.

On Feb. 5, CNN announced its decision. Well, part of it. CNN was hiring former Democratic vice presidential candidate Geraldine Ferraro to host *Crossfire* halftime. As the first woman on a major party's national ticket, she was a feminist icon. But Ferraro was a centrist who'd taken antiliberal stances on issues of race, religion and the death penalty.

CNN told reporters that Ferraro would share the job with one of five finalists still under consideration; the *Washington Post* identified them as "Democratic consultants Bob Beckel and Bob Shrum; Bill Press, chairman of the California Democratic Party; Jeff Cohen of Fairness and Accuracy In Reporting; and Juan Williams of the *Washington Post*."

Shrum would later co-pilot John Kerry's 2004 campaign, extending his streak in presidential campaigns to eight consecutive defeats. "[Shrum] helped to elect America's past four Republican presidents," reported the *Washington Post*. "Unfortunately, he did it while working for Democratic candidates." Beckel ran the 1984 Mondale-Ferraro campaign that carried one state out of 50, and then went on to a more successful career in corporate lobbying, as noted earlier.

Juan Williams gained notoriety among liberals through a 1991 *Crossfire* appearance in which he and Pat Buchanan both defended rightwing Supreme Court nominee Clarence Thomas. It was Williams, not Buchanan, who wrote that "liberals have become abusive monsters"—and who denounced "mob action" against Thomas by "so-called champions of fairness: liberal politicians, unions, civil rights groups and women's organizations."

A day after Ferraro's hiring was announced, Knight-Ridder TV writer Marc Gunther weighed in with a column—"*Crossfire* Lacks the Left, Despite Addition of Ferraro." He wrote that CNN should hire "a bona fide leftwing activist, the equivalent of Novak, Sununu and their predecessor, Pat Buchanan, who all are strong forces for the right. Of the remaining candidates, only one fits that mold: Jeff Cohen." Referring to Williams and Beckel as "Washington insiders" and Shrum as "a political consultant . . . in the thick of the corrupt and corrupting system of campaign fundraising," Gunther wrote:

> I caught a couple of [Cohen's] appearances on *Crossfire*, and
> he was a strong voice, able to mix it up with the pugnacious
> Novak—once taking an unpopular stance against the death
> penalty, another time mounting an impassioned defense of the
> feminist movement. Cohen's a populist, unafraid to take on the
> political and corporate establishment. In other words, he brings
> a point of view to television that isn't often heard.

CNN's choice mattered, according to Gunther, because *Crossfire* is "more important than most of the chat shows" and "actually can educate by focusing on a single topic each night."

★ ★ ★

But it was not to be. I return to the narrative offered by the inimitable Jim Hightower:

> The show's producers ran Jeff through the hoops, gave him a
> couple of tryouts, made positive noises about his professionalism,
> insisted that he was a finalist, and generally built up the boy's
> hope. Then they discarded him like a used hankie. It seems all
> they really wanted, from the get go, was someone to defend
> Bill Clinton.

Complaining that "Bill Clinton is as far left as the corporatized media is willing to allow the televised right-left dialogue to go," Hightower continued:

No Jeff Cohen, who would push the show's rightwing gang to the wall on the job-destroying impacts of NAFTA, on welfare for the privileged, on big-money corruption of the two-party system, on the crushing of America's middle class, on the growing health-care gap between those at the top and America's workaday major-ity . . . issues that no Clinton defender can hammer.

After mentioning the hiring of Geraldine Ferraro—a "cautious big-business Democrat" who would keep the debate "safe"—Hightower wrote:

OK, her name has some marquee value that Cohen doesn't, but then *Crossfire* announced it would name a second host to bolster the left's ranks on the show. And the winner was: Bill Press. Hardly a household name, even in his own household, but another safe choice for the powers-that-be.

What rankled Hightower is that Press—"California Democratic Party chairman at the time, totally dedicated to the big-money corpo-rate politics that dominates the party"—made a pledge to defend the "Clinton agenda" on *Crossfire* every night:

In case you are not quite clear on what that agenda might be, Press explained to the *Los Angeles Times* that Clinton represents a new Democratic effort to reposition the party away from a defender of the have-nots and into a party for the haves: "We have to reshape our agenda and stress the issues that appeal to the haves, like welfare reform and maybe some marginal kind of health reform, but no big, global thing," said *Crossfire*'s latest liberal hope.

★ ★ ★

I was disappointed but not surprised by CNN's choice. Fantasies of prominence and power had danced ever so briefly in my head. But I'm eternally thankful to CNN—its decision not to hire me forced a re-assessment of my and my family's future. It meant I'd have more time at home. Within days, my wife and I decided to have our second child. Any fleeting thoughts of "what coulda been" swiftly transmute into smiles for what is: my ebullient daughter Cady (nicknamed after feminist and abolitionist Elizabeth Cady Stanton). So much more than a consolation prize!

★ ★ ★

Postscript: Ferraro left *Crossfire* within two years to run for Senate (losing in the primary). CNN had to decide whether to have Bill Press host every night or find a Ferraro replacement to share the job with Press. Big names were bandied about in the media, such as former governors Mario Cuomo and Ann Richards.

My name was included only once as a possible replacement—in a Matt Drudge Internet item that asked if CNN would finally give me "a national forum."

CNN would not, sticking with Press full-time. But much to my surprise, Rupert Murdoch and a new thing called "Fox News Channel" would.

# PART II
# FOX NEWS

# CHAPTER THREE
## MURDOCH'S MEDIA CRITIC

I was never naive about Fox News Channel. It was launched in the fall of 1996 by rightwing media mogul Rupert Murdoch in his own image. I knew that he'd hired as his "news chairman" Roger Ailes, a GOP operative who was executive producer of Rush Limbaugh's TV show. I knew that Fox's first national "news anchor" was Tony Snow, a GOP operative who was Limbaugh's substitute on radio. What I did not know, until I'd been there a while, is that Ailes and Snow were "moderates" in the Fox News spectrum.

Ailes might seem an odd choice for news chairman, since he had virtually no background in journalism. But he was the perfect choice to run a partisan propaganda outlet. No one understands television—and its political uses—better than Ailes. He was a media Svengali behind the winning presidential campaigns of Nixon in 1968 and Reagan and Bush in the 1980s. Before there was Karl Rove (Bush Jr.'s Brain), there was Roger Ailes (Bush Sr.'s Fist).

I met Ailes once at a Fox News holiday party. If you knew nothing about him, this short, pudgy, balding fellow might appear cuddly, almost huggable, like a nice old uncle you'd nickname Jolly Roger.

Looks can be deceiving. Ailes was the media consultant for Bush Sr.'s vicious 1988 campaign that linked Democratic candidate Mike Dukakis to black rapist Willie Horton. "The only question," Ailes remarked, "is whether we depict Willie Horton with a knife in his hand or without it." Lee Atwater, his partner in the campaign, said that Ailes has "two speeds—attack and destroy."

Jolly Roger speaks; mogul Murdoch beams.

So Rupert Murdoch was putting Ailes in charge of a TV network during the reign of Bill Clinton, whom Ailes scorned as "the hippie president." Given his genius with 30-second TV attack ads, imagine what Ailes could do 24/7.

★ ★ ★

Shortly before the channel launched, I read that Ailes was planning a *Crossfire* knockoff on Fox in primetime. The show was to be centered around Sean Hannity, a rising rightwing talk radio star—with the working title "Hannity & Liberal to Be Determined." I heard that auditions were occurring.

By 1996, I'd caught a small dose of the TV pundit bug—so much money, so little time and so much potential influence. It began dawning on me that someone might actually pay me to pontificate; instead of just criticizing the limited spectrum of TV debates, maybe I could do something about it. Almost as a lark, I sent Fox News a video reel of my co-host appearances on *Crossfire* and expressed interest in the job.

I knew I was a long shot at Fox: If I was too daring for CNN, I was unlikely to fit on a show set up to give Hannity a platform. Ailes didn't want a fair fight; he wanted a nightly mugging. I never got a call.

It turns out that Hannity had personally nominated talk radio host Alan Colmes as his sidekick—a "former standup comic," according to the press. Colmes got the job. In my years of watching, Colmes has yet to make me laugh once.

Don't get me wrong: Alan Colmes is a nice guy who wouldn't harm a fly. But in echoes of Kinsley, when asked to place himself on the political spectrum, Colmes told *USA Today* in 1995, "I'm quite moderate." By contrast, Hannity is a passionate political proselytizer, telegenic and a self-described "arch-conservative."

From early on, the show was referred to by folks at Fox—on the air and off—as "the Hannity show" or simply "Hannity." I never once heard it called "the Colmes show." It was widely understood at Fox that Colmes' role was akin to that of the Washington Generals—the team sent out night after night to play the Harlem Globetrotters . . . and lose.

I heard that a top Fox News executive praised Colmes as the network's best host because "Alan knows what his job is . . . to make Hannity look good."

★ ★ ★

Two months after the channel launched, I made a guest appearance on *Hannity & Colmes* to debate President Clinton's comment that talk radio was overwhelmingly rightwing and vitriolic. Hannity, Colmes and the conservative guest were all active-duty talk radio hosts. As I settled into my seat, I expected as little support from Colmes as I'd received from Kinsley. I got less. While I identified the corporate interests behind talk radio's bias, Colmes was reluctant to say a bad word about the industry. The debate became a shoutfest pitting me against Hannity and the other rightwing talk host, who denounced me as a "pseudo-intellectual"—and, worse, "boring."

Howard Kurtz described *Hannity & Colmes* in the *Washington Post* as "*Crossfire* on speed." Hannity might have been on speed—with Colmes, it was more like Quaaludes.

★ ★ ★

A month after U.S. forces invaded Iraq in 2003, one of the co-hosts of *Hannity & Colmes* actually posed the following question: "Now that the war in Iraq is all but over, should the people in Hollywood who opposed the president admit they were wrong?" It wasn't Hannity.

## FAIR, BALANCED AND RADICALLY CONSERVATIVE

For years, columnist Norman Solomon and I have awarded annual prizes to highlight the foulest media performances of the year. We call them "P.U.-litzers." In 1994, we gave Rupert Murdoch the prize for "Media Hypocrite of the Year." Soon after acquiring Star TV, a satellite network broadcasting throughout Asia, Murdoch had lauded the democratic power of new media technologies as a "threat to totalitarian regimes everywhere. Satellite broadcasting makes it possible for information-hungry residents of many closed societies to bypass state-controlled television."

But when the Chinese government complained about Star's transmission of BBC news coverage of Beijing and human rights abuses, Murdoch obligingly removed the BBC from broadcasts to China. Too bad for "information-hungry" Chinese.*

Born in Australia, Murdoch was an old-style media mogul—dictatorial, imperial. He was also a modern mogul, the first to go global, using his media properties across many continents to boost conservative politicians—and not just in China. When he started buying up media outlets in the United States in the 1980s, *Cosmopolitan* asked Murdoch to what extent his conservative politics "influence the editorial posture of your newspapers." His reply: "Considerably. The buck stops on my desk. My editors have input, but I make final decisions. However, I don't see myself as a conservative so much as a radical. Maybe you'd call me a radical conservative." (In 1988, Murdoch told a top aide that he favored presidential candidate Rev. Pat Robertson: "He's right on all the issues.")

After hiring Ailes, the radical conservative owner would have little reason to meddle in the political posture of Fox News.

★　★　★

In its first months, Fox News Channel had few viewers and few guests willing to appear—especially guests not in sympathy with the rightwing enterprise. I got many invitations to appear and turned down most. When I said yes, it was largely because I was so darn curious to see what Ailes was cooking up in Murdoch's kitchen.

It struck me that Ailes' concoction was a glitzy TV version of the *New York Post*. The once proud, liberal paper had been acquired by Murdoch as his flagship U.S. daily; it served up a mix of rightwing politics and tabloid-style celebrity and crime coverage.

Under Murdoch, the *Post* was known for using its "news" coverage to assist Republican candidates, as in 1998 during the reelection bid of

---

* Soon after Murdoch purged the BBC from Star TV, the satellite system added the GE-owned CNBC channel (as part of a deal to get GE/NBC to shelve its FCC complaint over Murdoch's Fox TV being foreign owned.) Reuters reported that Star and NBC were confident that CNBC would not "upset edgy regional governments" and quoted an NBC executive: "There won't be any content that is sensitive in China."

New York's GOP senator Al D'Amato. When the newspaper's tracking poll found D'Amato ahead of Democratic challenger Chuck Schumer by 1.3 percent (less than the poll's margin of error), the *Post* made it front-page news with a banner headline: "AL STORMS AHEAD." But days earlier, the same poll had Schumer ahead by 4.2 percent; the *Post* put it at the bottom of an inside page, below the headline "Chuck squeaks ahead of Al in poll." (That day's front page was taken up by an endorsement of D'Amato.) Despite the *Post*'s help, storming D'Amato ended up losing by nine points to squeaking Schumer.

Fox News would continue this tradition of boosting Republican candidates—but with more success. Fox helped George W. Bush enormously in both 2000 and 2004. TV is a more powerful, less cerebral medium for propaganda than print, especially in Ailes' hands. From the beginning, you could see that Fox News had a faster pace than the rest of TV news, with revved up sound and graphics and headlines.

It also had a powerful slogan, "Fair and Balanced"—short and sweet, like a political campaign slogan. Ailes knew campaigning. It was media criticism and an attack line as marketing strategy: *We're balanced; our opponents aren't.*

No slogan in TV news history has been more disputed—prompting charges of consumer fraud, a lawsuit challenging its right to trademark the motto and a documentary (*Outfoxed*) largely devoted to debunking it. But Fox pounds its "Fair and Balanced" slogan harder than the junkman pounds his fender.

## ON MURDOCH'S PAYROLL

In 1997, six months after Fox launched, I became a paid pundit there—a panelist on the weekend show *Fox News Watch*. It felt strange to collect even a small check from Murdoch, a symbol of all that was wrong with corporate media. But I was appearing as a spokesperson for FAIR, offering the unvarnished FAIR critique week after week.

*News Watch* would become a more engaging and more critical media show than CNN's *Reliable Sources*. Whereas CNN shied away from FAIR representatives as regulars, usually preferring a traditional center-right debate, Fox actually welcomed us, knowing it made for more exciting television.

But truth be told, my permanent post at Fox had fluky beginnings—owing in large part to the quirky first host of *News Watch*, Eric Breindel. He'd been the editorial page editor of the *New York Post*, with a passion for 1950s-style anticommunist jihad. More important for me, Breindel relished debating genuine leftists and not just wimpy liberals. (Off the air, he loved debating the 1950s and my contention that executed "Soviet A-bomb spy" Ethel Rosenberg was not guilty.)

He also had the weirdest TV presence since *Saturday Night Live*'s Church Lady—halting, stammering, repeatedly interrupting even rightwing panelists. He had trouble reading the teleprompter. Tapings had to be stopped and restarted. The show's launch was repeatedly delayed because "the second floor"—Ailes and the brass—demanded more rehearsals.

We on the panel wondered why Ailes didn't just fire Breindel and hire a professional host. Then we figured it out: Ailes couldn't. Breindel was higher in the corporate hierarchy than Ailes. He was a senior vice president of Murdoch's News Corporation, which owned Fox— and a trusted political adviser to Rupert himself.

When *Fox News Watch* was finally allowed on air, *Hollywood Reporter* wrote that Breindel "isn't camera-friendly and looks awkward and frightened by the lens aimed at him." After several months, Breindel's health deteriorated and he seemed to be on pain-killers during tapings. When he died of an undisclosed disease at age 42, the *News Watch* staff attended his huge memorial service—along with Murdoch, Henry Kissinger, Mayor Giuliani, Governor Pataki and Senators D'Amato and Daniel Moynihan.

My TV career had been solidly launched, and it owed more to Breindel, this unusual rightwing ideologue, than any "CNN liberal."

★ ★ ★

Fox News Channel hired a top staff that was undeniably conservative. The week Fox launched, a report in the *Village Voice* indicated that potential employees were being asked their political affiliation, whether Democrat or Republican—an odd query for a TV news job. According to the *Voice*, when an experienced TV reporter refused to answer, "all employment discussion ended."

In fairness to Fox, I know of a producer who was hired after admitting to Democratic leanings. Maybe management kept a closer eye on him.

Over the years, I found Fox grunts (low-level producers and book-ers) to be little different—politically or otherwise—from those at CNN or MSNBC. But there was something distinctly different about Fox's higher-ups and on-air "talent." Even the weather and sports guys were fervid rightists. At Fox, I saw a "news" anchor engage a leading rightwinger off the air on where conservatives should stand on immigration policy—a confab among comrades.

Once I got stuck alone in the Fox greenroom with a supposedly objective news anchor, who proceeded to expound on how "people don't understand that our nation is not a democracy but a republic." It was because of ignorance, I learned, that Americans believe they govern a democracy. I didn't argue, just let the anchor bend my ear.

But my mind wandered back to my high school days in a conservative Detroit suburb when I worked on a term paper about claims that Communists were using rock music and the Beatles to subvert America's youth. Research led me to a house near school where I could pick up primary source materials . . . published by the ultraright John Birch Society. Before I approached the house, my classmate warned me, "Whatever you do, don't let them know you're Jewish." Along with a tape on Ringo Starr's subversive drumming technique, I was handed a Birch Society pamphlet—*America Is a Republic, Not a Democracy.*

## *NEWS WATCH*

I survived the roiling seas of Fox News Channel only because the *News Watch* show acted as my lifeboat. Aboard that small, solitary weekend vessel, I could say and do things that would have sunk me anywhere else.

Over time, my *News Watch* gig became as sweet as one could be for a progressive at Fox. I savaged the corporate media week after week and got paid for it . . . by Darth Murdoch. Life doesn't get much better than that. I appeared as a panelist on the show about 200 times from 1997 through 2002.

*News Watch* was the smartest and most balanced show on Fox and perhaps anywhere on cable news. Admittedly, as I stated earlier, that's "a high jump over a low hurdle." Added provisos can be crucial. Like when my girlfriend told me years ago, "Jeff, you're the most feminist man I've ever met"—and as I beamed proudly, she added, "And that's the problem."

When Breindel died, hosting duties at *News Watch* were taken over by Eric Burns, a skilled TV interviewer who (oddly, for a Fox host) was welcoming to all viewpoints and made sure every panelist was heard.

The producer of *News Watch* was TV veteran Charlie Reina, the best producer I ever worked with—smart, fair in his treatment of all panelists, a clever writer of TV copy. (When Charlie left Fox in 2003, he blew the whistle on how Fox's bias reflects "management's politics." Fox predictably slammed his thoughtful criticism as the "rantings of a bitter, disgruntled former employee.")

One complaint I had about *News Watch* was topic selection. Almost any rightwing claim of bias could become a topic on our show, sometimes at the behest of Fox brass. And we did our share of tabloidy segments on Lewinsky, O.J., JonBenet, reality TV, school shootings—sometimes unavoidable given that we were a media show, commenting on what others in the business were obsessing upon. On the positive side, our show did more than any other on mainstream TV to criticize corporate media mergers, censorship, advertiser influence and journalists' coziness with their powerful sources. We had wide-ranging debates on coverage of war and elections. We analyzed sexism in reporting and coverage that deletes people of color from the news except as criminals, drug dealers or illegal aliens.

Another concern I had at *News Watch* was the tilt of our cast. The show started with a domineering rightwing host plus a three-person panel: *National Review* editor John O'Sullivan on the right, *Los Angeles Times* media writer and savvy journalism professor Jane Hall in the center and me (or a FAIR colleague) on the left. Given the heavy-handed host, our lineup clearly tilted right—in other words, "fair and balanced" in the Fox sense.

When centrist Eric Burns became host, our show became truly balanced—with panelists who let each other talk. At Fox, that wouldn't last long. Viewers complained. There was a sense that John O'Sullivan, an affable Brit, wasn't combative enough from the right.

After a while, John was gone. Taking his place was columnist Jim Pinkerton, a fierce debater more prone to interrupt (or Commie-bait) fellow panelists. As head of opposition research for Bush Sr.'s 1988 campaign, he had promoted Willie Horton and the Pledge of Allegiance as attack themes. Pinkerton was six-foot-nine-inches tall, but no gentle giant in the ring. In fact, he was all elbows, a master of gratuitous aside-swipes. Discussing a 1960s-related topic, he'd say, "When you were burning American flags in the '60s, Jeff. . . ."

This cast—Eric, Pinkerton, Jane and me—lasted about a year. What I enjoyed about debating Pinkerton is that, like Bob Novak on *Crossfire*, his views were sometimes so extreme that I sounded commonsensical by comparison. Pinkerton often found himself isolated on the panel: No matter how deep into the gutter a media outlet was shown to be in pursuit of profit, his unshakeable mantra—"let the marketplace decide"—would have us shaking our heads.

I regularly challenged Pinkerton's notion that our corporatized media system was a marketplace serving the public. In 2002, when ABC tried to lure David Letterman from CBS to replace Ted Koppel's *Nightline*, I commented:

> This idea that there's somehow a marketplace working is a myth. *Nightline* . . . isn't in danger because of a small audience. It's actually got more viewers than Letterman. But [Koppel] doesn't have enough of the young males that advertisers prefer. . . . So it's a marketplace that doesn't serve the consumer. It's a marketplace for the advertisers.

After Pinkerton joined *News Watch*, some viewers still complained that the show was "too liberal." We were joined by a new cast member, conservative megapundit Cal Thomas. He'd evolved from Moral Majority spokesman to the most widely syndicated columnist in the country; if you read newspapers, you've probably seen his mustachioed mug in one of the hundreds of dailies that carry his column. Cal didn't replace the existing rightwinger; he was *in addition*. This lineup would last for years: Cal and Pinkerton on the right, Jane and

*News Watch* cast: Eric, Jane, Pinkerton, me, Cal

Eric more or less in the center and me alone on the left.

I found the first weeks of this lineup excruciating. On political issues, I was outgunned, unable to respond effectively to GOP spin coming from two directions. When I complained off the air about the imbalance, I was told that I should be flattered: If I weren't such a good debater, they wouldn't need two conservatives on *News Watch*. And I should be thankful Fox hadn't taken the quicker path toward a "fair and balanced" tilt—firing me.

★  ★  ★

Over the years, our team developed *esprit de corps*, as friendships formed across ideological lines. Even Pinkerton grew on me, despite his often eccentric views. He insisted, for example, that candidates for public office—from city council on up—must be willing to answer any and all media questions about their sex lives.

On one show, Jane lost her admirable patience with Pinkerton, pointed her finger at him, and declared, "If I were one of these politicians, I'd say, 'What about your sex life?'" Taking Jane's side, I needled, "What about yours, Jim? You've got a lot of power, more than any city council member. Why don't we ask you about your sex life?" Pinkerton just laughed. A commercial break saved him from further questioning.

At times our show was sufficiently convivial that panelists would forego an ideological retort in favor of a clever punch line. Days after the 2000 election, I was railing against the campaign coverage: "Gore's puny personal embellishments were blown into big stories. But George Bush, on the campaign trail and in the debates, was making willful distortions of his own record—taking credit for bills that he obstructed or vetoed or watered down on issues from taxes to the patients' bill of rights."

When I finished venting, Cal simply quipped, "Hey, if you can't distort your own record, what can you distort?"

Some of my progressive friends were appalled by my friendly relations with Cal, seen by them as a Religious Right bully. But I saw some integrity and wit, and Mom taught me to look for the best in people. On politics, we rarely agreed. But Cal (who'd been an NBC reporter) and I were often in unison on *News Watch* in criticizing the impact of media conglomerates on TV news—conflicts of interest, sensationalism, reporting cutbacks, bottom-line mentality. This put Cal at odds with Pinkerton's "let the marketplace decide" outlook.

My standard response to Pinkerton was that there's hardly a "marketplace" in an industry dominated by a half-dozen firms. Conglomerates don't compete; they collude.

# BITING THE HAND

During my tenure on *News Watch*, I criticized Fox News or Murdoch or Murdoch outlets dozens of times. I prided myself on it. I would have quit had anyone told me I couldn't act on my instinct to bite the hand that feeds me (when it deserved biting).

I took Fox News to task on high crimes, like aiding George W. Bush's ride to the White House. And misdemeanors, like hiring Geraldo Rivera as a war correspondent—I called him "buffoonish." Sometimes I went after Murdoch for simple sleaze, like running photos of nude women ("Page 3 Girls" or "Page 3 Lesbians") each day in *The Sun*, England's biggest newspaper.

In 1999, on the eve of Prince Edward's wedding, Murdoch's daily tabloid caused a stir by publishing an old photo of the bride with her breast exposed. (Murdoch's nickname in England: "Dirty Digger.") We discussed the incident on *News Watch*. Since the segment setup didn't mention the paper's owner, I did.

> COHEN: *The Sun*, which is owned by Rupert Murdoch, is a "conservative" newspaper that has used naked women to puff up its profits for a long time. I think there's a contradiction there.
>
> PINKERTON: What's the contradiction?
>
> COHEN: What's the contradiction? Conservatives talk about family values, traditional values while exploiting women for big money.
>
> PINKERTON: *The Sun* has their own definition of family values.

Unfortunately, Pinkerton never got a chance to explain. I'm no prude, but it is indeed strange that the media mogul who's done the most to whip up Bush's religious conservative army is a soft-core pornographer—a fact largely unknown by that army.

★ ★ ★

In June 1999, during a *News Watch* discussion on the 10th anniversary of the massacre of students at Tiananmen Square, I blamed soft media coverage of China's government on the economic interests of firms like Murdoch's News Corporation:

Some of the biggest media conglomerates really want access to the Chinese market—U.S. media conglomerates, whether it's News Corporation that owns this channel or Disney or General Electric that owns NBC. They want in there and they've been willing to go along with the government and sometimes suppress news about human rights violations in China in order to keep their contracts and relationships.

Months earlier, as News Corp. prepared to open its Beijing office, Murdoch was asked if his conscience bothered him over stifling criticism of China at his various media outlets (like a Murdoch publishing house that had recently dropped a book critical of China): "Not for a moment, no. I'm the head of the company," said the mogul. "It's my responsibility sometimes to interfere."*

★   ★   ★

Going after Fox for assist to Bush in 2000

On our first *News Watch* after the 2000 election, during the recount furor, I had yet another reason to attack Fox News. With Florida too close to call on election night, Fox decided at 2:16 Wednesday morning to be the first network to declare Bush the winner of the state and therefore the country. Within four minutes, the other TV networks all followed Fox's lead. The call was wrong; Fox and the other red-faced networks retracted it within two hours.

_____

*In News Corp.'s 1999 annual report, Murdoch waxed eloquent about one planet, indivisible, under Rupert: "Our reach is unmatched around the world. We're reaching people from the moment they wake up until they fall asleep. We give them their morning weather and traffic reports through our television outlets around the world. We enlighten and entertain them with such newspapers as the *New York Post* and [London] *Times* as they have breakfast, or take the train to work. We update their stock prices and give them the world's biggest news stories every day through such news channels as Fox or Sky News. . . . Before going to bed, we give them the latest news, and then they can crawl into bed with one of our best-selling novels from HarperCollins."

But the damage—in shaping the public view of Bush as the winner—had been done.

It gets worse. Fox News had hired Bush's first cousin, John Ellis, to head its election-night decision desk. It was Bush's cousin who recommended calling Florida for Bush. The *New Yorker* quoted Ellis as boasting that "everyone followed us." (Ellis, a conservative columnist, had crunched election numbers years earlier for NBC.)

Before Fox told its viewers the good "news" about Florida, Ellis had personally informed cousins George and "Jebbie": "It was just the three of us guys handing the phone back and forth," Ellis explained. "Me with the numbers, one of them a governor, the other the president-elect. Now that was cool." Throughout Election Day, wrote the *New Yorker*, Ellis had "stayed in constant touch with his cousins in Austin, relaying early vote counts as they showed up on his screens." Ellis told the magazine, "Jebbie'll be calling me like 8,000 times a day."

On *News Watch*, I challenged the company line that the Ellis episode didn't amount to much: "It mattered that Fox News was the first network that called not only Florida for Bush, but the country for Bush. It created this image that Bush was the presumed president and Gore is trying to snatch something." (Day after day, Hannity was accusing Gore and the Democrats of trying to "steal the election.")

And I questioned why Ellis had been hired in the first place:

> Sixteen months before the election, John Ellis was writing a column for the *Boston Globe*, and he told his readers he didn't want to cover the presidential campaign anymore because of his cousin, George W. Bush. He says, "I'm for him today, I'm for him tomorrow, I'm for him as long as he's running for office. On some level, I can't be honest about his campaign. My loyalty goes to him and not to you, the reader." Now having said that you believe yourself to be too partisan to write even an opinion column, what appearance does it give if you hire him to do objective numbers crunching?

★  ★  ★

On a couple occasions, a *News Watch* topic related to Murdoch or Fox News, and producer Charlie Reina could glean from preshow conversations that virtually every panelist believed Murdoch or Fox deserved criticism. Before the taping, we'd get a pep talk from Charlie: "Guys, I know your views on this. Don't let Jeff be the only one who speaks out."

We'd go on the air . . . and I'd find myself all alone, teeing off on Murdoch or Fox. Political prudence was never my strong suit—which may explain why I'm no longer on TV.

★ ★ ★

I wasn't alone in seeing *News Watch* as a bright star in the general bleakness of Fox News Channel. In a raucous 2001 *Vanity Fair* piece depicting Fox News as a bully pulpit for the Republican Right, critic James Wolcott singled out our show for praise. He described *News Watch* as "sharper and more creatively angled than CNN's *Reliable Sources*, one of Fox's beat cops being Jeff Cohen of Fairness & Accuracy In Reporting (FAIR), who's farther to the left than any other talking head on cable."

Wolcott continued: "Cohen's presence is a credit to Fox News, even if he is outnumbered by one-note johnnies Cal Thomas and Jim Pinkerton, syndicated columnists who appear to keep their brains in a jar between broadcasts."

Ouch!

On the next *News Watch*, as Eric Burns read the Wolcott quote during our viewer mail segment, Cal and Pinkerton good-naturedly held up jars. As far as I could tell, there was no brain matter in them.*

Brains in a jar?

## NO SPIN ZONE

The undisputed star of Fox News Channel is Bill O'Reilly. At the beginning, no one recognized that fact except him. There were higher-profile folks like Tony Snow, or Brit Hume from ABC, or Catherine

---

*Wolcott's piece also skewered Fox's faux liberals like NPR's Juan Williams (formerly a CNN liberal). Wolcott worried that "Williams is going to walk into the Washington studio one day as a black man and walk out a disgruntled honky"— and that columnist–Fox panelist Jeff Birnbaum was "gravitating so far to the right he'll soon be sitting on Fred Barnes' lap."

Crier, who'd been at ABC and CNN. But O'Reilly—who'd anchored the tabloid show *Inside Edition*—always seemed to view himself as the network's star and expected to be treated as such by those around him. When his ratings climbed, he got his wish.

O'Reilly had a swaggering gait even while seated. An imposing TV presence, his face exudes emotion—annoyance, frustration, fury—better than most TV actors. He had an intimidating presence at Fox, like the schoolyard bully; I always thought he'd just received too few hugs along the way.

I appeared as his guest about eight times. Most of my appearances were cordial, often embarrassingly so. The best thing about appearing with O'Reilly is that it's usually one on one—no other guests. That could also be the worst thing, when his temper erupted and you're out there alone. He calls his show "The No Spin Zone." But seated across from him, I sometimes felt like I was inside a tilt-a-whirl cup in overdrive, holding on for dear life.

O'Reilly is a roaring contradiction: abundantly bright but meagerly informed. A strong debater and interrogator, but consistently underprepared. A voice of the little guy who treats those around him as inferiors. A voice of morality who made lewd phone calls to a female employee (and was apparently caught on tape doing so).

In the first year of Fox, I was given two solo segments on O'Reilly's show to discuss my book *Wizards of Media Oz*—during which he endorsed my detailed critique of an "establishment media" too cozy with corporate and political elites. It was obvious O'Reilly hadn't taken the time to examine the book, much of which contradicted his most cherished views.

In February 2000, his producers booked me to talk about my *Los Angeles Times* column on media hero worship of GOP presidential aspirant John McCain. I was thrilled to be discussing my controversial piece that questioned whether it was heroic of McCain to bomb Vietnam—and argued that the reverential treatment of the largely conservative McCain debunked the myth of a liberal press corps. I looked forward to going at it with O'Reilly. But once the segment began, it was fairly evident he hadn't read the 700-word column. There were no fireworks.

Initially I passed off his cursory research as laziness. But I came to see that it had more to do with his (at least subconscious) sense that research and inquiry might erode his beliefs. With O'Reilly, his beliefs are bedrock, immovable. Everything else—facts, logic, perhaps someone's jaw—can be rearranged.

★ ★ ★

My worst blowout with O'Reilly occurred during the frenzy of the November 2000 Florida recount. My goal during the appearance was to confront several media myths then circulating. One was a Nixon myth, brandished to lecture Gore: *Why don't you put the country first, like Richard Nixon did in 1960, and not challenge the Florida tally in court?* I pointed out on O'Reilly's show that while the 1960 election "wasn't even close compared to this," the Nixon forces did indeed pursue court challenges.

O'Reilly was ferocious in insisting that Nixon's people made legal challenges only "because they were setting up a run four years from then." He and I went back and forth—not quite getting each other's point.

O'Reilly also got revved up when I confronted the myth that the number of disqualified ballots in Palm Beach County had been "normal" in 2000 and no big problem. I pointed out that the number of

Florida 2000: I depart; he debates.

overvotes for president (ballots apparently marked twice) and undervotes (apparently unmarked ballots) had actually been "twice as high as in 1996." Palm Beach election officials had found 30,000 disqualified ballots in 2000—thanks in part to the confusing butterfly ballot—way up from only about 14,000 in 1996. O'Reilly wrongly claimed that the numbers were similar from 1996 to 2000.

After we went off the air, our to and fro continued a while. I felt I'd better leave before he threw me out of the studio.

I rushed out of the building, jumped into a cab and called a friend to ask what he thought of the stand-off. But he started yelling at me, "Are you watching it?"

"Watching it?" I replied. "It's over."

"Well, O'Reilly's not over," my friend said. "He's still talking about you!"

Sure enough. O'Reilly had cut into his next segment (with rightwinger Laura Ingraham) to continue the debate with me . . . except I was downtown in a cab. His commentary began "A couple of clarifications with the Jeff Cohen segment, for those of you keeping score." He then went on at length, again inaccurately, to minimize the amount of disqualified ballots in Palm Beach in 2000—and offered a short retort about Nixon.

★ ★ ★

After our Florida recount brawl, I was sure I'd never appear again on *The O'Reilly Factor*. I was surely wrong.

To O'Reilly, I was good television. Ten weeks later I was invited back into the zone. The *National Enquirer* had published an evidence-free article about Bill Clinton and the wife of fugitive businessman Marc Rich, whom Clinton had recently pardoned. So there I was again—me and O'Reilly and a segment headlined "Did Denise Rich and Bill Clinton Have an Affair?" No one at Fox was as perfectly attuned as O'Reilly to the Murdochian mix of tabloidism and rightwing politics.

O'Reilly opened the segment on Clinton's alleged affair by saying, "This story was thin, didn't have any on-the-record sources."

I corrected him: "I'd say it's less than thin. It's nearly invisible." As we discussed the baseless claim, I complained that the *Enquirer* had "succeeded in getting us here to discuss this story, even though they brought no evidence to the table."

"That's what a free press is all about," O'Reilly retorted.

When I noted the pattern of supermarket tabloid stories getting covered "in the 24-hour news cycle" of Fox News and CNN, O'Reilly changed the subject to Juanita Broaddrick's charge that she'd been raped in 1978 by Clinton, at the time attorney general of Arkansas. O'Reilly asserted that the story "was spiked by the major media primarily." To which I responded, "But the reporter who got it to prime-time was at NBC."

Left unrebutted, O'Reilly could be dangerous. In Los Angeles weeks earlier, O'Reilly had made a similar but more specific charge against the *L.A. Times*. As quoted in *MediaWeek*, O'Reilly claimed the newspaper "never mentioned Juanita Broaddrick's name, ever. The whole area out here has no idea what's going on, unless you watch my show."

Informed later that O'Reilly was way wrong and that the *L. A. Times* had repeatedly mentioned Broaddrick, the *MediaWeek* writer explained that she might have caught the error "if I hadn't been so mesmerized by O'Reilly's sheer O'Reillyness. There's just something about a man who's always sure he's right even when he's wrong."

★　★　★

I'm convinced O'Reilly isn't faking it when he portrays himself as a victim of sneering elitists. His persecution complex is genuine. He was under fire in March 2001 when I appeared with him on the *National Enquirer* nonstory.

Self-conscious over having anchored the tabloid *Inside Edition*, O'Reilly had long asserted that the show had won a Peabody, "the highest award in journalism." But the day before my O'Reilly appearance, Al Franken pointed out in the *Washington Post* that *Inside Edition* never won a Peabody. It had won a Polk Award, and that for an exposé done *after* O'Reilly left the show.

The next day, Michael Kinsley's column skewered O'Reilly over his claims of being a working-class hero persecuted by snobs. Among other debunkings, Kinsley noted that when O'Reilly says his dad, an accountant for an oil company, "never made more than $35,000," that's $100,000 or more in today's dollars.

Before our segment began, I asked O'Reilly about the incoming fire he was receiving. Macho Bill brushed it off, seeming only a little rattled: "They'll need more than that to come after me."

★　★　★

At the beginning of Fox News, I expected O'Reilly to crash and burn by whipping himself up and saying something so outrageous on air that even Fox would have to fire him. But after his ratings climbed, he became an untouchable. He could say or do anything—without repercussion.

Like when he called for punishing civilians six days after 9/11: "The U.S. should bomb the Afghan infrastructure to rubble—the airport, the power plants, their water facilities, and the roads. . . . The Afghans are responsible for the Taliban. We should not target civilians.

But if they don't rise up against this criminal government, they starve, period." To O'Reilly, it didn't matter who had attacked us—many would have to pay: The Iraqi "infrastructure must be destroyed and the population made to endure yet another round of intense pain." Same with Libya: "We mine the harbor in Tripoli. Nothing goes in, nothing goes out. We also destroy all the airports in Libya. Let them eat sand."

When O'Reilly bears a grudge, the gloves are off—as are the facts. After a friendly guest mentioned that some "nutcase" bloggers believe that President Bush "orchestrated the 9/11 attacks," O'Reilly responded, "You mean he didn't? That's what I've been hearing from Phil Donahue . . . and Michael Moore—that he orchestrated it." As O'Reilly knew well, Donahue and Moore have said nothing of the kind.

None of O'Reilly's wild claims undermine his position with Fox management. Especially this one: "I'll submit to you that George W. Bush is the closest modern president to what the Founding Fathers have in mind."

Or this one on Bush foreign policy and invading Iraq: "I'm telling you that President Bush is doing just what Jesus would have done."

It didn't hurt that O'Reilly could be a company flack—in October 2003, he boasted about Fox's coverage of the Iraq war: "I think Fox News Channel was lucky because we were less skeptical of the war, and the war went very well. So we won."*

## WE OPINE. YOU RECLINE.

I thought a lot about Fox's audience. Over the years, dozens of strangers recognized me from the channel and approached me. I was startled by how often they had a supermarket tabloid under their arms. Once, a slightly creepy Fox viewer followed me into an airport men's room, shouting after me, "Are you a socialist?"—while my daughter Sequoia waited apprehensively at the door.

Politically, most Fox viewers seem close to your typical, conservative talk radio fan. Intellectually, perhaps a cut below that, maybe a bit lazier—TV, after all, provides the pictures.

---

*In an email read on *News Watch,* an Oklahoma viewer wrote, "Jeff Cohen is the only real intellectual on the entire Fox News Channel. I'd love to see him play a round of *Jeopardy* against Bill O'Reilly or George Dubya."

A massive 2003 study by the University of Maryland's Program on International Policy Attitudes found that Americans who got their news from commercial TV were confused about basic facts related to the Iraq war. Most held at least one of three "misperceptions": that Iraq was tied to Al Qaeda, that weapons of mass destruction had been found in Iraq or that global public opinion favored the U.S. invasion of Iraq. Viewers of Fox News were the most misinformed of all.

★ ★ ★

I'm frequently asked how many Fox staffers actually believe the "fair and balanced" rhetoric. In my experience, it's a small percentage—primarily true believers like anchor Brit Hume (who I'll get to shortly).

The sharper folks inside Fox take the slogan with a big grain of salt. I can remember occasions at Fox when a one-sided Fox story on the greenroom TV would prompt someone to quip, "Well, that was sure 'fair and balanced'!"—leading to titters all around from staff and contributors. When Tony Snow left Fox in April 2006 to become President Bush's spokesman, a Fox pundit deadpanned, "It'll be good to have a fair and balanced press secretary."

But I give Roger Ailes credit. As a marketing slogan, "fair and balanced" is sheer genius because it works simultaneously with two broad audiences: (1) those who are so uninformed about news and current events that they might actually believe it and (2) those who understand the slogan largely as rhetoric, but rhetoric they want to hear. These viewers watch Fox because it appeals to their biases. But like voters who want to support a candidate who shares their prejudices (say, against gays or blacks), many are happier supporting a candidate who communicates in code, rather than one who is overtly prejudiced. Hence, the soothing "fair and balanced" rhetoric works— as shared pretense—even for Fox's hardcore conservative base, a base recruited from day one by ads airing on radio talkshows like Rush Limbaugh's.

Many conservative viewers understand that Fox is hardly more "fair and balanced" than Limbaugh himself. Thanks to campus lectures in so-called red states, I've met many devoted young Fox viewers—but very few who see the channel as unbiased.

★ ★ ★

It's not easy to come up with a slogan more insincere than "fair and balanced." Fox News accomplished that with "We Report. You Decide."—which insinuates: *While our competitors lay their ideology on you, we give you just the facts, ma'am.* This one is absurd because no TV news operation offers more punditry and less reporting than Fox. (Paying a pundit to bloviate is cheaper than hiring reporters to dig up the news.) A more accurate slogan would be "We Opine. You Recline."

★  ★  ★

Let's end this chapter with some candor from William Kristol, a Fox luminary and editor of Murdoch's rightwing *Weekly Standard*. A year before Fox News launched, Kristol remarked, "I admit it, the liberal media were never that powerful, and the whole thing was often used as an excuse by conservatives for conservative failures."

# CHAPTER FOUR
## FAIR AND BALANCED

Think it's impossible to find a TV news executive who makes Roger Ailes look liberal? Meet John Moody, a former *Time* correspondent hired by Ailes as his lieutenant, Fox's senior news vice president. In Moody's view, his *Time* colleagues were not merely liberals; they were Commie-symps who were "drawn ideologically, romantically, theoretically, to the side of the Sandinistas"—the leftist revolutionaries who governed Nicaragua in the 1980s.

To hear Moody tell it, the problem is not that he's rightwing. It's that elite journalists hired by Time Warner, GE and other conglomerates are so irredeemably leftwing. As he told *Brill's Content*:

> There's a certain sameness to the news on the Big Three and CNN.
> . . . America is bad, corporations are bad, animal species should be
> protected, and every cop is a racist killer. That's where "fair and
> balanced" comes in. We don't think all corporations are bad, every
> forest should be saved, every government program is good. We're
> going to be more inquisitive.

So how does an inquisitive news executive instruct his staff in the art of being "fair and balanced"? Through an often opinionated daily memo on what stories to cover—and, in some cases, how to slant them. The e-memos frequently identify the political good guys and bad guys. One warned Fox staffers to expect "whining" from antiwar protesters about Iraqi civilian casualties. Another labeled remarks by UN chief Kofi Annan "utterly incomprehensible."

When Bush went to Egypt to meet Arab allies in June 2003, Moody enthused that Bush's "political courage and tactical cunning are worth noting in our reporting through the day." In March 2004, with the

Bush White House obstructing the commission investigating 9/11, Moody advised, "Do not turn this into Watergate."

As U.S. troops prepared to move into the Iraqi town of Fallujah in 2004, Moody gave firm instructions: "We will cover this hour by hour today, explaining repeatedly why it is happening. It won't be long before some people start to decry the use of 'excessive force.' We won't be among that group." Two days later, Moody wrote, "Do not fall into the easy trap of mourning the loss of U.S. lives and asking out loud why are we there?"

During the 2004 campaign, Moody seemed to gloat when he wrote that John Kerry's "coarse description of his opponents has cast a lurid glow over the campaign." A few days later, he noted that Kerry was "starting to feel the heat for his flip-flop voting record."

No one has come forward with a Moody memo instructing staffers to impute a sinister French-ness to candidate Kerry, but it became a Fox mantra. Kerry was not just a flip-flopping, soft-on-defense liberal—he was also a candidate who looked French, talked French, acted French and, if not rejected by voters, "would be America's first French president," as a Fox host put it.

When I was at Fox, I'd heard about Moody's daily memo (which went to staffers, not contributors), but copies didn't start circulating publicly and on the Internet until the 2004 release of the movie *Outfoxed: Rupert Murdoch's War on Journalism*. Before that, the only public mention of the memo had come from our *News Watch* producer-turned-whistle-blower, Charlie Reina, who survived six years full-time at Fox (after a career at CBS, Associated Press and ABC).

In an October 2003 letter posted on a journalism website after leaving Fox, Reina wrote that Moody's daily memo was "born with the Bush administration early in 2001," ensuring that the White House line came through loud and clear: "At the Fair and Balanced network, everyone knows management's point of view, and, in case they're not sure how to get it on air, The Memo is there to remind them." Noting that Fox is "nonunion," Reina stated, "With no protections regarding what they can be made to do, there is undue motivation to please the big boss."

★  ★  ★

I met Moody only once, a brief and slightly incoherent meeting in May 2001. The face-to-face was prompted by a FAIR Action Alert criticizing Fox News. By then, I had left FAIR's staff and had no role in the group's day-to-day decision-making. I hadn't seen the email that infuriated Moody until he and the rest of the public saw it.

FAIR's alert, "Irresistible Lies," documented how Fox—in the days after the White House handover from Clinton to Bush II—had repeatedly and feverishly reported that departing Clinton staffers had "trashed" or "vandalized" the White House and Air Force One.

Sean Hannity spoke of the Clintonites stripping "anything that was not bolted down on *Air Force One*—$200,000 in furniture taken out." Brit Hume relied on a gossipy rightwing column to report that *Air Force One* "was stripped bare. The plane's porcelain, china . . . and silverware, and salt and pepper shakers, blankets and pillow cases, nearly all items bearing the presidential seal were taken by Clinton staffers."

Other outlets had reported the vandalism claims. But on Fox, the coverage was indignant and prosecutorial on show after show. If Fox's charges were true, viewers could only feel huge relief that the Bush grown-ups had rescued the White House from Clinton's juvenile delinquents.

There was only one problem: The charges *weren't* true. So said the agency that manages the White House and *Air Force One*. FAIR had caught Fox red-handed (or "red-pawed"). FAIR encouraged its activists to ask Fox why "anonymous reports backed with no evidence became a major focus of their transition coverage."*

I was summoned to Moody's second-floor office from the greenroom on a day we were taping *News Watch*. He seemed annoyed, not looking at me, staring off to the side—a bit like Captain Queeg in *The Caine Mutiny*. The meeting started badly (with him implying I was lying about my reduced role at FAIR) and got worse: "Was it *fair* to single out Fox?" he asked. "Were we the only ones who covered this?"

"No," I replied. "FAIR's approach is to target the outlet that best exemplifies a particular bias. The *New York Times*, ABC, Pacifica Radio have all been recent—"

"What do you mean by *target*?" he interrupted.

"FAIR doesn't threaten or intimidate anyone," I said. "It focuses attention on specific outlets over specific biases. Check the archive and you'll find more alerts this year aimed at the *New York Times* than anyone."

---

*On *News Watch*, I remarked that "in the first week of the Bush administration, one of the first acts was to deceive journalists. And I'm surprised there isn't more looking at how they got deceived . . . what this says about the Bush administration."

Now he was in total disbelief: "So you're saying you focus on the most liberal newspaper in the country!"

To Moody, it seemed impossible that one of those outlets swarming with Sandinista-lovers might have any bias that would concern FAIR. Nor was he buying that FAIR's "targeting" was anything less than in-

FOX: THE MOST BIASED NAME IN NEWS

timidation. He appeared to be expecting an apology. I offered none. I did suggest he write FAIR a response for publication.

"Then you'd probably come at us again," he countered. I didn't argue the point. Nor when he said, "I guess we don't have anything to say to each other."

I walked out.

This was one of the only periods I felt close to losing my job at Fox. But six weeks later, FAIR released a thorough and devastating report titled *Fox: The Most Biased Name in News*, which received big coverage in the mainstream press. That exposé may well have saved my job. If they fired me now, it would appear to be retaliation over FAIR's critical report on Fox—which would bring even more attention to FAIR's criticism.

★   ★   ★

Long after my meeting with Moody, I learned why he might have been especially sensitive to criticism of Fox's role in the White House–trashing hoax: He had helped instigate the coverage. In a memo to his troops in January 2001, Moody wrote:

> The outgoing [Clinton] administration's outrageous conduct is worth following. The episodes—they are too serious to dismiss as pranks—should be listed on a full screen and put up EACH HOUR, along with live shots or guest segs. Mancow referred to it this morning as the "white trashing of the White House."

You may be wondering who (or what) is "Mancow," quoted approvingly by Moody. He's a frothing radio shock jock from Chicago and a Fox News regular who literally spat his rightwing commentary into a close-up camera. After Paula Zahn left Fox for CNN and was savaged for it by Ailes in the press, Mancow did a skit on Fox's morning show in which he repeatedly hit an actor portraying Zahn in the face and screamed, "I'll kill you, Paula! We will kill you, Paula!"

Cable news or pro wrestling? You decide.

# TRUE BRIT

My favorite "fair and balanced" anchor is Brit Hume, known for his Republican leanings when he covered Washington as a top ABC News correspondent under Reagan, Bush I and Clinton (while writing articles for rightwing journals). As host of *Special Report with Brit Hume*—Fox's signature political news show at 6 o'clock every evening—he helps shape the channel's agenda even before polemicists like O'Reilly and Hannity come out after dark. Hume, of course, is presented as a straight news guy, Fox's "managing editor."

Raised amid privilege and private school in Washington, D.C., Hume doesn't pretend to O'Reillyesque man-of-the-people populism. Soon after the July 7, 2005, terrorist attacks in London, Hume told Fox viewers, "My first thought when I heard—just on a personal basis, when I heard there had been this attack and I saw the futures this morning, which were really in the tank, I thought, 'Hmmm, time to buy.'"

Hume is no bleeding heart. A running theme of his Iraq war coverage has been how historically "minor" are U.S. troop casualties. When the number of U.S. deaths in Iraq reached 2,000, Hume remarked, "By historic standards, these casualties are negligible." Once Hume sought to downplay casualties by saying that "U.S. soldiers have less of a chance of dying" in Iraq "than citizens have of being murdered in California, which is roughly the same geographical area." The claim was preposterous and the geographic comparison meaningless—since the state's population is hundreds of times larger than the number of soldiers in Iraq. (If Californians were being murdered at the rate of U.S. deaths in Iraq, its murder rate would have soared from 6 per day to 400.)*

---

*Brit's wife, Fox's D.C. bureau chief Kim Hume, is no bleeding heart, either. She told *New York* magazine that Fox tends to ignore the stories favored by the journalistic establishment, which are "all mushy, like AIDS, or all silly, like Head Start. They want to give publicity to people they think are doing good."

As part of its exposé of Fox News, FAIR surveyed Hume's guest list for the first 19 weeks of 2001 and found something unprecedented in television news: For every Democratic partisan featured in an interview segment, there were more than eight Republican partisans. That's 89 percent Rs vs. only 11 percent Ds.

Contrary to the Fox party line that the channel's bias is an optical illusion (appearing conservative only "because the other guys are so far to the left," as Ailes tells it), previous studies had consistently found that other national news shows also favored Rs over Ds, but only slightly. As a control for its Hume study, FAIR surveyed CNN's *Wolf Blitzer Reports* during the same 19-week period: Blitzer favored R over D partisans by 57 to 43 percent.

When the *New York Times* interviewed Hume about FAIR's study and the extraordinary eight-to-one Republican bias, he did a Mr. Magoo impression—acting as if he'd never noticed any slant in his program's guest list: If "we find that there is some imbalance," Hume said, "then we'll correct it."

In cooperation with the *Outfoxed* documentary, FAIR updated its study in late 2003 by reviewing 25 more weeks of Hume's program. The new results: Rs outnumbered Ds by five to one.

From an eight-to-one GOP bias to a mere five-to-one bias. I'd departed Fox by then, but I could picture a Moody email going to Hume: "Hey, Brit, what's with this lurch to the left?"

★  ★  ★

Brit Hume and I tangle.

My only on-air appearance with Hume occurred in 1999 when he was a guest panelist on *News Watch*. Our panels, unlike Hume's, offered a real diversity of views, which seemed more than he could handle. That week's topic was a Freedom Forum poll—conducted after the "all Monica, all the time" frenzy—in which most respondents said the press had "too much freedom" and a large minority said the media are "harmful to democracy."

"Look at what happened throughout 1998," I commented, "when the Washington pundit elite was just obsessing on this story of Monicagate. . . . The ratings popularity that Clinton had, that were going up, were a rejection of the media . . . a backlash against the media."

Hume turned the discussion from the poll's findings to his complaint that the poll missed the big issue—the large number of people who feel "the media are politically biased." Hume went on: "To some extent, this network—Fox News Channel—was founded on the premise that we are where you can come if you believe the media are biased left and want to see it played straight down the middle."

He said "straight down the middle" with a straight face.

I mentioned other polling that showed increasing numbers of Americans who think the media favor conservatives, and many who believe the media are too soft on corporate owners and advertisers. Hume started talking over me. He was incredulous: "You getting majorities for that, Jeff?"

COHEN: You're getting 80 or 90 percent: "Do you believe that the media are being influenced by owners, by advertisers?"

HUME: Eighty or 90 percent of whom? The editorial staff of *Mother Jones*?

Actually, a nationwide Roper survey of 1,500 people in 1997 (written up in a *Parade* magazine cover story) found that 88 percent of respondents said they believe corporate owners improperly influenced news reporting, while 90 percent said the same about advertisers.

Hume's ignorance is equaled only by his arrogance. Night after night, he signs off by saying, "Stay tuned to Fox News: Fair, balanced and unafraid." He's not joking.

★ ★ ★

In 1999, Fox News was unafraid of a tabloid story that President Clinton had fathered a "love child" with an African American prostitute 13 years earlier. The story had knocked around the Clinton-hating fringe for years without breaking into the mainstream.

But after Special Prosecutor Ken Starr published Clinton's DNA profile, the *Star* supermarket tabloid arranged a DNA test on the child in question. Rightwing Internet gossip Matt Drudge (then a Fox News host) broke the story big on his website . . . *before any test results*. This sparked front-page coverage in the *New York Post* and repeated mention on Fox News. While even the supermarket tabloid sat on the story pending the test results, Murdoch's media soldiers were propelling it across several continents.

The results of the DNA test? Negative. The story was apparently a big hoax. But it had reached millions thanks to Murdoch's echo chamber.

On Fox News, I repeatedly blasted Fox, Drudge and the *Post* for promoting the story. During a *News Watch* debate on whether mainstream media should cover a supermarket tabloid story alleging an affair involving Gov. Jeb Bush and Florida's Republican secretary of state Katherine Harris, Pinkerton argued that if true, it should be covered. I frowned on the story but added, "If this was about Democratic politicians, I believe history shows that Drudge or the *New York Post* or Fox News would somehow elevate it into the mainstream, like they did that very phony story about Clinton and an illegitimate child."

★ ★ ★

In 2001, Jon Stewart and Comedy Central's *Daily Show* received a Peabody Award—the same award that O'Reilly claimed his tabloid show had won. A Peabody is granted for excellence in television (without specific categories). In accepting the award, Stewart joked that he had won in the "News Parody" category: "There was not much competition this year. It was just us and Fox."

## LET THEM BURN!

Every so often, *Fox News Watch* would include a guest or substitute panelist. It was fitting that one of our first guest panelists was Bill O'Reilly. Having emerged as the network's star by 1998, O'Reilly came on to promote his novel about a fired TV news anchor who exacts revenge by savagely murdering network executives. (Is there a psychiatrist in the house?) I tried to read it but couldn't get beyond the blood and guts that saturate the book's opening pages.

His appearance on *News Watch* offers a reminder that it took O'Reilly a while at Fox to find his steady rightwing voice. Initially, his primetime rants were *not* confined to liberal targets on the approved Murdoch/Ailes/Moody enemies list. I remember O'Reilly railing against greed in healthcare and proposing a salary cap of $400,000 or so on physicians—who, he said, should be in the profession to heal and not to get rich. I could imagine a Moody memo carping at O'Reilly's "creeping socialism."

During our remarkably amicable discussion of TV news on *News Watch*, O'Reilly seemed to be stealing my lines: "Unfortunately, most people get their news from television these days," he said. "But television is a business. Their primary focus is not informing the people. It's making money."

O'Reilly complained about "subtle dishonesty" in TV news: "It's not what you hear; it's what you don't hear. 'That's going to threaten the corporate structure, so I'm not going to report that story.' Or, 'that's a little too blue-collar, and here in New York, we don't mingle with those kinds of people. We're not going to report that story.'"

Since that *News Watch* appearance, Blue-Collar Bill has waged holy crusades against war critics, the ACLU, Jesse Jackson, Cindy Sheehan and so many others. But "the corporate structure" has been safely sheltered from his wrath . . . in some sort of "no-sin zone."

★ ★ ★

My favorite *News Watch* substitute on the right was Liz Trotta, a network TV news veteran who ended her career, fittingly, at the Rev. Moon–owned *Washington Times*. She was apparently a friend of Moody's and became a Fox News contributor. Once when I was a *Crossfire* guest, supreme ideologue Bob Novak wailed at me, "You're so heavily ideologized, Mr. Cohen, that you don't know what you're talking about!" I sometimes felt like yelling that at Trotta.

I did lose my cool with her on occasion, as when we were discussing Ted Kaczynski, an academic dropout who pled guilty to being the Unabomber terrorist who'd dispatched mail bombs to scientists and academics. The bomb spree began after Kaczynski moved to a shack in the Montana woods without electricity or running water, where he lived as a recluse, tracking animals and eating wild plants. In the anti-technology manifesto that led to his capture, Kaczynski attacked leftists and feminists and belittled environmentalists.

But rightwingers like Trotta tried hard to link the Unabomber to environmentalists and the left. On *News Watch*, she complained that "mainstream media coverage tried to divorce Kaczynski's background and milieu from what he became."

I went ballistic. "He lived as a hermit since the 1970s," I yelped. "For 25 years, the guy lived in a shack and you're talking about his *milieu!*"

★　★　★

With Trotta you never knew what would come out of her mouth—a bit like Ann Coulter, but without the miniskirt. On a 2002 *News Watch*, we discussed a Harry Potter book-burning jamboree organized by a New Mexico preacher. Muggles, please read to the end.

> COHEN: Censorship and ignorance walk hand in hand. I mean, the pastor said he hadn't read any of the [Harry Potter] books; he hasn't seen the movie. I mentioned this story to my daughter who's 10 and has read all of the books; she thought it was idiotic. She knows that witchcraft is imaginary. But a lot of parents like these books because if you take away the metaphor of wizardry, what you have is books that extol friendship and working hard and studying hard and courage. I think these are wonderful books for kids. It's funny that the pastor didn't bother—he's proud that he hasn't even looked at the books.

> ERIC BURNS: But you know that's a fairly common thing, Liz. People who denounce—I remember the movie some years ago, *Last Temptation of Christ* by Martin Scorsese—there was a huge protest movement undertaken by someone who had not read the screenplay and not seen the movie. Shouldn't you not admit that, if you're going to go to the extreme of—

> LIZ TROTTA: Absolutely. But what are we talking about? We're talking about the press getting hysterical over some, you know, two-bit book-burning. Let them burn!

Book-burning? No big deal. Flag-burning? Amend the Constitution to ban it.

# UNCIVIL LIBERTIES

I've long been a proud supporter of the American Civil Liberties Union. On *News Watch*, I boasted more than once of having been an ACLU lawyer. Boasting of ACLU loyalties on Fox News is like boasting of veganism on the Food Channel.

ACLU-bashing is deeply rooted at Fox—starting with boss Roger Ailes, who helped run Bush Sr.'s 1988 campaign that repeatedly derided Dukakis as a "card-carrying ACLU member." O'Reilly has called the ACLU a "fascist" group that uses "tactics the Taliban would admire" (ironically, because it challenges state sponsorship of religion).

Fox regularly crusades on air against the alleged "war on Christmas"—waged by "ACLU America-haters," in O'Reilly's words—that has bullied much of America into saying "Happy Holidays" instead of "Merry Christmas." (Even the fearless Fox News was apparently intimidated: They sent me one season's greeting card after another that *never* mentioned Christmas, with Roger Ailes' handwritten note offering a wimpy "*Happy Holidays.*")

One of John Moody's memos conveyed his "fair and balanced" view of the ACLU. After the hotel that housed Fox's Baghdad bureau was hit by an explosive, Moody wrote that Fox personnel were OK and urged prayers "of thanks for their safety to whatever God you revere (and let the ACLU stick it where the sun don't shine)."

Not to be left out of the chorus, Sean Hannity has disparaged co-host Alan Colmes for being a "card-carrying member of the ACLU."

So imagine my surprise at being told by my friend Carol Sobel that, as a lawyer for the Southern California ACLU, she'd represented Hannity. It turns out that Hannity's broadcasting career began as a volunteer talk radio host at a Santa Barbara college station, and it nearly ended when he lost his show after making bigoted comments about gays and telling a lesbian mother, "I feel sorry for your child."

Who did Hannity turn to when his free speech was threatened? The ACLU, an organization that for 85 years has courageously defended American heroes and patriots. It's also defended Nazis, Klansmen, Hannity and fellow Fox News host Ollie North.

★ ★ ★

Being a regular pundit on TV news during the 9/11 crisis was difficult, especially at Fox News, where American flag lapel pins sprouted

faster than poppies in post-Taliban Afghanistan. The usual media lockstep about U.S. military action and all things "national security" got even more intense. TV hosts who were volatile in normal times erupted in calls for revenge against whole Middle Eastern populations.

I encouraged sobriety. A colleague and I suggested that *News Watch* panelists wear sport coats instead of our normal shirtsleeves, as a quiet show of respect for the victims. On our first show after the attacks—a day in which Fox's "America United" banner was prominent—I criticized the hysterical comments of pundits like Ann Coulter and noted that some commentators seemed to be competing over "who could call for the killing of more innocent people abroad." I won rare backing from fellow panelist Jim Pinkerton.

> COHEN: Some of the punditry was almost a mirror image—in bloodlust and fanaticism—of what the terrorists on the other side of the globe say.
>
> PINKERTON: I actually agree with Jeff in substantial measure on this. I watched Bill Bennett on CNN saying—here's our chance to take out Iraq, Iran, Syria, Libya *and* China.
>
> ERIC BURNS: How did China get in there?
>
> PINKERTON: I don't know. Ask Bennett.
>
> COHEN: I think it was a competition over who could throw in the most countries.

As our nation headed toward war abroad, while restricting civil liberties at home, I repeatedly invoked the separation of press and state: "Journalists in a democracy owe their loyalty to the public, not the government." In a time of war, I said, "The most patriotic thing a journalist can do is his or her job—tell it fully, tell it accurately, ask the tough questions." I was a lonely and unheeded voice.

When U.S. forces started bombing Afghanistan, I urged journalists to express their patriotism through hard-hitting questions of the White House, unlike what most did in the early years of Vietnam—a war that wouldn't have withstood media scrutiny: "Because the media went into the tank, we ended up with a fiasco in Vietnam. If this war is more justified, then let it stand up to journalistic scrutiny."

Such talk irritated Pinkerton. His response was to declare Vietnam "Jeff's favorite war, because America lost." When Pinkerton challenged my patriotism for raising questions about the "war on terror," I asked if he was un-American when he (along with Hannity) opposed Clinton's Kosovo war. That was somehow different.

★  ★  ★

Like the rightwing pundits who've used Fox News to grind their ideological axes over the years, my status as a weekly panelist allowed me to bang the drum for my pet causes. I plugged FAIR's website so many times on *News Watch* that it became a running gag, with fellow panelists sometimes mentioning FAIR.org to preempt me. I was able to regularly praise independent outlets, such as Amy Goodman's *Democracy Now!*, CommonDreams.org, AlterNet and *The Nation*. I pushed serious reforms, like free TV time for candidates, including credible third-party candidates—and whimsical reforms, such as Jim Hightower's proposal that politicians (like NASCAR drivers) wear the logos of their corporate sponsors on their suits.

If Pinkerton had his "let the marketplace decide" mantra, I had a few of my own. On news media going tabloid: *Occasional diversion is a good thing; perpetual distraction is not.* On media adulation of celebrities: *The flip side of media worship of celebrities is media contempt for working people.* On the corporate takeover of news: *Conglomerates are using the news media as weapons of mass distraction.*

★  ★  ★

I'm often asked how I lasted five years at Fox without getting fired. It's a question I frequently ask myself. Unlike many Fox News liberals who are conciliatory and tend, à la the Washington Generals, to make the Hannitys of the channel look good, I was a loud and unyielding foe of the whole Fox ideology.

I think there were two factors behind my survival.

1.  I was primarily a weekender. There was more tolerance for me than if I'd been a regular in primetime when the audience is many times bigger. The stakes are lower on weekends, forbearance higher—especially on a show whose special purpose was media criticism.

2.  I give good television. *News Watch* received more viewer email about me than any panelist. People were watching in part because my persistent polarizing with Pinkerton or Cal Thomas, or both, created sparks. From the voluminous email, it was clear that many watched the show because I was the guy they loved to hate. For some others, I was the guy they loved to love—perhaps the entire 17 percent of Fox viewers who are liberal or progressive.

For a select group of women, obviously very lonely ones, it was more lust than love. Without fail, their emails were read on air. One gave me a nickname that stuck (at least in the greenroom): "Hottie." Another wrote that while our views clashed, my smile was hard to resist. Ideology mattered more than looks to a Texas woman: "Jeff is such a handsome sexy man, especially when he keeps his mouth shut."

My physical presence was not so dazzling to conservative men: "Lift some weights," wrote one angry emailer, "and get some shoulders, please."

## GREENROOM FOLLIES

Being a regular in TV news means spending quality time in the greenroom, the waiting area where people hang out before airtime, next to the makeup rooms. (And, no, it's not usually green). On Fridays at Fox News headquarters in New York—with weekend shows being taped, as live shows were airing—the Studio C greenroom could resemble a three-ring circus, peopled at various times by anchors, authors, actors, politicians, porn stars, pro wrestlers, rabbis, supermodels and *News Watch* panelists getting ready for show time.

With the biggest (and loudest) panel, the *News Watch* team tended to rule the roost in the greenroom for an hour each Friday. Sometimes Sean Hannity would dash through for makeup before a midday segment. A couple times, he got an earful from my colleagues, goading him: *Sean, why don't you have Jeff as a co-host? Afraid of him?*

"It's a great idea," Hannity responded, saying he'd propose it for the next time Colmes took days off. He was a bit too enthusiastic to be believed. "Hannity & Cohen" never happened. I was little more than a weekender, not ready for primetime hosting.

Once Michael Moore saw me in the greenroom and made a big show of berating me as a "sell-out" for being a Fox regular and taking Murdoch's money. He was kidding, of course. His publisher at the time was Murdoch's HarperCollins.

Sometimes a late-breaking topic would be added minutes before a *News Watch* taping, and panelists would scurry around the greenroom to grab whatever newspapers were there. Quality dailies might not be around, but there were usually plenty of copies of the *New York Post*, a Murdoch outlet housed in the same building. I wasn't the only one whose attitude was *It's in the* Post—*how do we know it's true?*

The realm of Murdoch came in for ribbing in the greenroom— much safer than saying it on air. Once while I was bantering with a colleague about Murdoch's love affair with China's rulers and his censoring of critical news, almost unnoticed in the corner of the room appeared John Cleese of Monty Python. Cleese muttered some wisecrack under his breath about Murdoch and his new bride. The 68-year-old mogul had married a 32-year-old Chinese-born woman, an executive at Murdoch's Star TV—soon after divorcing his wife of 32 years. ("Murdoch and his beautiful bride," gushed a *New York Post* photo caption, "only have eyes for each other.")

★　★　★

For a while, the show that taped right before ours (and usually ran late) was hosted by powerful Murdoch publishing executive Judith Regan, one of the top women in her industry. The show's original title: *That Regan Woman.* She interviewed eclectic guests, but I couldn't help noticing that many were Murdoch authors. Call it corporate synergy.

Regan was less synergistic with subordinates. One day, as I entered the usually jovial greenroom, it felt more like a morgue. I thought someone had died. No one was speaking above a whisper. "What's happened?" I quietly inquired. I learned that the day before, in the middle of the night, several Fox makeup artists and hair stylists had been yanked out of bed to face questions from New York police *homicide* detectives. One culprit was in New Jersey. What murder were they suspected of? Well, not exactly a murder. The interrogations of sleepy-eyed Fox employees were prompted by a missing cell phone—Judith Regan's.

Given the level of crime in New York (and anxiety weeks after 9/11), the extraordinary attention paid to a missing phone was inexplicable. Except perhaps that New York police chief Bernie Kerik was one of Regan's authors . . . and her lover. Call it corporate-cop synergy.

Three years later, Kerik was President Bush's nominee to head the Department of Homeland Security—until scandal over his personal and business life forced him to withdraw. That's too bad. Imagine if the same meticulous security afforded this one Murdoch publisher could have been extended to our entire homeland.

★ ★ ★

Of the many illustrious folks I was able to say hello to in the Fox greenroom, there was no greater thrill—or incongruity—than bumping into Gore Vidal (whom I'd come to know because of his support for FAIR). We spoke briefly after he guested on Regan's show. Much later I saw Vidal's description of Fox News as "Fox Zoo, in which you have a number of people who pretend to be journalists but are really like animals. Each one has his own noise—there's the donkey who brays, there's the pig who squeals. . . . They don't want the people to know anything, and the people don't."

## CABLE NEWS CRACKUP

Media are the nervous system of our body politic. If the nervous system is misfiring, our democracy is jeopardized because the public is not warned of dangers requiring urgent action. Beginning in May 2001, cable news suffered a total nervous breakdown. It lasted four months.

During that period, John Ashcroft's Justice Department was devoting major resources to surveil prostitutes in New Orleans and medical marijuana clinics in California, while rebuffing (on Sept. 10, 2001) the FBI's request for $58 million in additional counterterrorism funds for more agents, analysts and interpreters.

During that period, Defense Secretary Donald Rumsfeld was demanding billions of dollars in "Star Wars" funding to defend America from ballistic missiles, while threatening a presidential veto (on Sept. 9, 2001) over a Senate proposal to shift $600 million from space-based weapons systems to counterterrorism.

During that period, 19 Al Qaeda terrorists—including two on the CIA terrorist watch list—were deploying across our country, while Zacarias Moussaoui was arrested in Minneapolis due to suspicious behavior at a flight school, and George W. Bush received a presidential briefing memo titled "Bin Laden Determined to Strike in U.S."

During that period, the synapses of cable news crackled overtime, to the point of nervous exhaustion. Instead of warning the body politic about real threats in our immediate environment, cable news had trouble focusing on anything other than one sham menace. Psychiatrists might call it a pathological or hallucinatory or paranoid obsession.

That one menace was Gary Condit, a previously obscure Democratic congressman who remained ineptly tight-lipped as he was ritualistically skewered by the media. Condit—54 and married (to one woman since age 19)—had a relationship with a former D.C. intern, 24-year-old Chandra Levy, who disappeared in May. There is zero evidence Condit was involved in her disappearance. He was never a police suspect. A year after her disappearance, Levy's skeletal remains were found in a Washington, D.C., park where she'd been jogging, an apparent victim of random crime.

From May to Sept. 11, abetted by the tailwind of Clinton-Lewinsky, cable news covered no story more than Condit-Levy. Not the stagnant economy, not California's energy crisis, not Bush's tax breaks benefiting the well-off, not Ashcroft's or Rumsfeld's misguided priorities, and certainly not something or someone named Al Qaeda. Al who?

On Sept. 11, Osama bin Laden became the most despised man in America. In the previous months, Gary Condit had been the most despised man in America—especially on cable news, where he was linked week after week to murder, without need of evidence. Night after night, cable news fluffed its ratings with tales of Condit's sex life. He was no more corrupt with power, sexual or otherwise, than other congressmen. But he was intimate with the wrong woman at the wrong time—and the media nailed his ass to a high-tech scaffold with a capital (and scarlet) *A*.

For cable news, it was the perfect tabloid storm—adultery, murder, mystery—with no end to speculation on how Condit might have played a role in Levy's disappearance. Perhaps Levy died during rough sex with the congressman. Or her death was connected to Condit's ex-con brother. Or Condit's buddies in a motorcycle gang. Or because Levy was pregnant with Condit's baby.

"TV's barking heads are drooling," wrote media critic Todd Gitlin.

The story was propelled much more by salacious interest in Condit's sex life than concern for a missing woman. A cable viewer could hear thirdhand claims about his alleged S&M practices, homosexual fantasies, leather fetishism.

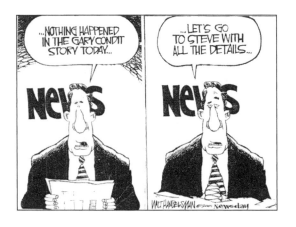

Newspapers also fed the frenzy. The *Washington Post* published a page 1 exclusive about an alleged affair Condit had years earlier with a teenage girl. The story was based on the girl's father, a minister, who later admitted he concocted the tale. The *New York Post* quoted an alleged Condit sex partner gossiping about the gossip she'd read; 10 days before terrorists would attack New York, Murdoch's *Post* quoted the woman as saying, "When we did the whole handcuff and blindfold thing, it was soft stuff—not the serious S&M stuff I've read he's gotten into now."

Amid the conjecture that filled hundreds of hours of cable news, Paula Zahn on Fox News interviewed a "world-renowned psychic" from California, who asserted that Chandra Levy's body was in a D.C. park by "some trees down in a marshy area." The following excerpt gives a bit of the flavor of the interview.

> PSYCHIC: This girl—I am sorry to tell you this, but this girl is not alive.
>
> ZAHN: How do you know that, Sylvia? Has this been something that you've been spending time thinking about and analyzing?
>
> PSYCHIC: No, no, no. Paula, you know, you can either be one place or the other. If you're not here, you've got to be there.
>
> ZAHN: And why are you so convinced she's there?
>
> PSYCHIC: Because I'm a psychic. I know where she—I know she's there. She was gone very quickly after she was first missing.

Ironically, the psychic's speculation turned out to be more accurate than much of what passed for informed analysis on the story.

★  ★  ★

In August 2001, *Broadcasting & Cable* reported, "Helped by the Chandra Levy mystery, Fox News Channel is continuing its ratings tear, besting CNN for the sixth consecutive month. Fox News' primetime ratings have climbed one-tenth of a point each month since the former intern vanished in May."

## GARY CONDIT AND ME

Gary Condit's public humiliation boosted many TV careers, including mine. Besides discussing Condit-Levy in segment after segment on *News Watch*, I was now pocketing extra checks whenever I appeared on Fox primetime shows. My role was peculiar. I was a well-paid party to the feeding frenzy, while constantly denouncing it.

Near the beginning of the Condit cable soap opera, I warned on *News Watch* that "if it turns out that Chandra is a victim of random street crime, I think some in the media are going to owe a Richard Jewell–type apology to Congressman Condit." (Jewell was the security guard who received payouts from news outlets that had suggested he planted the bomb at the Atlanta Olympics; the actual culprit was an ultraright terrorist.)

Sure enough, writer Dominick Dunne later gave Condit an apology and an undisclosed sum to settle a suit stemming from Dunne's fanciful thirdhand fable told on talk radio, CNN and elsewhere that Condit was involved in a Washington sex ring of Arab diplomats, which somehow led to Levy being kidnapped and dropped into the Atlantic Ocean from a private jet.

"In the dictionary, when you look up 'media circus,'" I said on *News Watch*, "you'll see a picture of Condit, and behind him Geraldo and O'Reilly and Larry King." I blasted the recurrent TV segments that asked, *Is there too much coverage of the Chandra Levy disappearance?*— which, I complained, was "a way of adding to the overkill, while pretending not to."

In August 2001, I was O'Reilly's top guest on a show focused heavily on Condit. O'Reilly opened the show by saying, "First off, I'm really tired of talking about the story, and I agree with Dan Rather that some of us in the TV news business have been shamelessly exploiting the Condit-Levy situation." After he and I discussed the ethics of a magazine examining Chandra Levy's sexual history, O'Reilly concluded the segment with an admission: "Many smart viewers are going to be saying, 'Hey, O'Reilly, you said you wouldn't report it, but you're discussing it with Jeff Cohen.'"

When Connie Chung of ABC News snagged an exclusive live interview with Condit in primetime, I was a featured analyst offering real-time commentary on a Fox News special hosted by Paula Zahn. My first comment, like almost every comment I made on the Condit case, attacked the coverage:

> In the months that talk television and cable news has wrung so many ratings, so many audiences, so many big shows out of this one story, we're supposed to say, "Well, it's about the disappearance. It's not about sex." But in the first 15 minutes of the Connie Chung interview, all she's asking about is: "Define the relationship."

I become part of the Condit horror show.

After the Chung interview in which Condit sidestepped her repeated questions about the nature of his affair with Chandra Levy, I remarked on *News Watch*, "What Condit didn't understand is that there's this smash hit entertainment series that's been going on all summer, and it's his sex life. And he wasn't cooperating."

On a Fox primetime show, I denounced "Condit-centric" media for "going down the toilet by stripping bare this public figure's private life for their own ratings."

Noting how all the "talking heads from the O.J. Simpson and Lewinksy stories" were returning to TV for the Condit case, I joked on air that I wouldn't be "satisfied until I hear from Tonya Harding"—the Olympic ice skater implicated in an assault on her top competitor. I soon got my wish: Larry King actually interviewed Harding about Condit. Hey, Larry, I was just kidding!*

★ ★ ★

I had become the Fox studio deodorizer. Bring out Jeff Cohen for five minutes to spew at the media for exploiting the story, and then plunge onward with hour after hour of tabloid stench, innuendo and sexploitation.

My FAIR colleagues and I first found ourselves sucked into this role soon after Princess Diana's car crash. We were invited on cable news shows to criticize the hypocrisy of respectable media sneering at the paparazzi for hounding Diana—while readily using the paparazzi's invasive, long-lens photos of her. Which would give cable news yet more opportunities to exhibit the photos, while we went on bellyaching. We'd become integrated into the horror show we were criticizing.

At the height of the Condifixion, rightwingers had the nerve to complain on Fox and elsewhere that "the liberal media" were not identifying Condit often enough as a Democrat. This was beyond silly. In December 2000, just months before Levy's disappearance, top Fox News pundits had warmly discussed Condit as a "conservative Democrat" being considered as a possible Bush cabinet member, perhaps secretary of agriculture. And have I mentioned that Condit joined in cosponsoring a rightwing Republican bill to put the Ten Commandments in public school classrooms?

During my last Fox primetime appearance about Condit in August 2001, an enraged pundit urged him to resign from Congress and "slither away and never be heard from again." My immediate response: "What's the mainstream media going to cover when he does go away?"

I would soon get my answer.

---

*During Conditmania, *News Watch* discussed a viewer's email that invoked Neil Postman's book, *Amusing Ourselves to Death*, on the dumbing-down impact of TV on democracy. I commented, "Neil Postman's book is prophetic. It's written in 1985—that's before JFK Jr.-O.J.-JonBenet-Chandra-Monica. And since 1985, the TV networks and TV news have been taken over by the entertainment conglomerates. . . . Look at the health of our democracy. Fewer people vote. Fewer people can identify their member of Congress. . . . News is soap opera; it's not about debate, policy, issues. That's dangerous to democracy."

Eighteen days later, U.S. intelligence picked up chatter from intercepted conversations among Al Qaeda members indicating an imminent attack: "tomorrow is zero hour" and "the match begins tomorrow." That night, cable news was offering its own chatter—the latest gossip on Condit.

The next morning, hijacked jets torpedoed the Twin Towers—wiping Condit's forgettable and banal image off of TV screens for good, replaced by the haunting visage of Bin Laden.

Never before had a "news" story of such absolute dominance disappeared so abruptly.

★ ★ ★

People assume I was fired by Fox News. Or that I walked away disgruntled. In fact, I was quite gruntled. I had grown to enjoy my weekly *News Watch* gig. I left on my own for what I thought was a better opportunity elsewhere in cable news. Immediately, I missed my Fox show and my colleagues there.

And *News Watch* apparently missed me. Host Eric Burns graciously informed viewers of my move to another network: "What Jeff brought to this program was courage and conviction, wit and knowledge. He made every conversation in which he took part more energetic, more interesting, more fair, more balanced."

I did not miss Ailes, Moody and those atop the channel. That's why I agreed to be interviewed for the movie *Outfoxed*, a powerful expose of Fox News bias. The documentary received strong press attention and was a sensation in Internet-driven grassroots marketing—a top-selling DVD on Amazon.com in July 2004.

In August 2004, I came to New York for an *Outfoxed* screening in connection with protests outside the Republican National Convention at Madison Square Garden. Fox News had rented a massive billboard opposite the Garden. Due to security, I wasn't able to get close to it, but I wondered if the fine print read, "Official TV Network of the 2004 GOP Convention."

★ ★ ★

When I left Fox after five years in May 2002 to join the middle-of-the-road cable outfit MSNBC, I was sure I'd get a better platform for my progressive views. Who knew I was better off at Fox?

# PART III
# MSNBC

# CHAPTER FIVE
## BELLY OF THE BEAST

Blame it on Phil Donahue, the luminous *secular* evangelist who got America thinking and talking issues on daytime television, nine-time Emmy Award winner, TV pioneer and America's most famous and best-liked liberal.

If it weren't for Phil, I would have remained at Fox News as house contrarian, working a few hours a week for a full-time income—spouting off on the sins of media evildoers, including Murdoch and Fox.

But I gave it up because Phil Donahue decided to come out of his happy retirement to give TV viewers an alternative to the raging hyenas dominating the airwaves. Like the New York radio host bellowing within hours of 9/11, "Bomb somebody, Goddamnit!" And Bill O'Reilly calling for starving Afghan civilians, destroying Iraq's civilian infrastructure and mining Libya's harbor: "Let them eat sand." And Ann Coulter urging, "We should invade their countries, kill their leaders and convert them to Christianity."

When Phil asked me to join forces with him, I found it hard to refuse—especially since I'd been urging him for months to make a TV comeback. I'd written a brief memo analyzing his limited options: public TV ("controversy averse"); syndication ("even Limbaugh failed"). Cable news seemed the best option: "CNN is in disarray, might be an opportunity for them to make an edgy choice. Fox News needs a liberal/progressive-hosted show."

I first met Phil as a repeat guest on his syndicated daytime show and his primetime CNBC program, *Pozner & Donahue*. When I tested for the *Crossfire* job, Phil touted me to CNN. In 2000, we were allies in trying to open up the dreary presidential debates to third-party candidates like Ralph Nader. And we worked closely post-9/11 in trying to communicate, above the media din, that *acting smart* against Islamist terrorists was more important than *acting tough*.

If anyone on the left could triumph in the timid and corporatized TV news environment, I felt it was Phil Donahue. Over three decades,

no one had done more to bring issues of feminism, gay rights, consumer rights and corporate responsibility to the American mainstream. Unlike today's hosts, Phil was known for respectful treatment of guests with opposing views. Ever entertaining, he had a record of attracting an audience.

In April 2002, the big news was announced: Phil Donahue was returning to TV to host a

Phil brought social issues to daytime TV.

primetime issues show that would run opposite Bill O'Reilly. He'd be appearing on MSNBC, the third-placed cable news channel owned by General Electric and Microsoft, and run by GE's NBC. *USA Today* headlined, "Donahue Set to Throw a Left Jab at O'Reilly." Press accounts had MSNBC turning to the "unabashed liberal" as a "bold move to lift the cable news channel's sagging ratings."

Soon after the news broke, I argued on *Fox News Watch* that an MSNBC Donahue show could succeed as counterprogramming against Fox conservatism:

> Fox News has sort of been niche programming, and it was aimed at and pitched to conservatives. And conservatives already dominated talk radio. . . . You can't beat Fox as Fox-lite. So a smart strategy would be Phil Donahue, who I know and like . . . a guy who speaks for millions of people who are voiceless.

A week later, at Phil's urging, I had a get-acquainted meeting with MSNBC. Days after that, Phil was exhorting me to join him at the struggling channel: "You need to fill your backpack and begin the long trek out of Fox darkness."

To this day, I'd follow Phil most anywhere. Anywhere except GE's dysfunctional TV news channel.

★  ★  ★

My first meeting with a top MSNBC executive went better than I ever could have hoped. And not just because we swapped Roger Ailes stories as we sipped drinks in a Manhattan bar. The MSNBC exec was entirely in unison with me that Phil's show must provide a stark alternative to Fox—unambiguous counterprogramming. I was delighted by what I heard. The show would be partisan and passionate like O'Reilly's (without abusing guests of course), but offering a totally opposite viewpoint.

I expressed interest in working with Phil behind-the-scenes on such a show, but I said that I wouldn't leave Fox unless I also had a strong on-air presence at MSNBC. His response took my breath away, though I tried not to show it. Not only could he guarantee me regular appearances as a contributor, but he told me that MSNBC was remaking its daytime lineup to include several left-right *Crossfire*-type debate shows and that it was likely I could co-host one of the shows each day. (In torrid email correspondence over the next weeks, my co-host job became a virtual certainty.)

I had come to the meeting from my home in Woodstock, New York—a scenic two-hour train ride along the majestic Hudson River south to New York City. The face-to-face was friendly from the outset, especially after the MSNBC executive broke the ice by asking me if GE was indeed "not telling the truth about the Hudson River." A GE plant had contaminated the river with toxic PCBs, and the company had used its political muscle to stall a cleanup for decades. It was a cute, offhand remark at the boss's expense, clearly meant to stay at the table. But he seemed to be signaling two serious points to me: (1) that he knew his corporate boss was capable of rank dishonesty and (2) that knowing something like that and ever saying it on the air or in public are two different propositions.

The lesson: Journalism is not quite a pursuit of truth, especially when the owner is involved.

## IF I'M DRUG-FREE, WHY DO I
## SEEM TO BE HALLUCINATING?

My life moved into warp speed, as I prepared to cut my cord with FAIR, the nonprofit I had birthed, and go behind enemy lines full-time. I was being offered my own afternoon show to co-host—and a "senior producer" job on *Donahue*, MSNBC's flagship primetime show. Two jobs in one and a salary several times bigger than I'd ever received, plus GE benefits. As I went into overdrive filling out the obligatory GE/NBC paperwork, I got a call from an MSNBC Human Resources staffer: "We need to arrange your drug test."

"You're joking, right?" I said

"No. It's GE company-wide policy," he told me.

Was I joining a news channel or a high school football team?

Suddenly, my hiring process slowed to a crawl. I'd long opposed employee drug tests on principle as invasions of privacy (with rare exceptions for public safety jobs). Living in Woodstock, even a nonuser can get a marijuana contact high just by association. And there was something especially troubling about journalists—supposedly intrepid, independent and protective of Constitutional freedoms—lining up to pee in a cup on command.

As I dawdled, MSNBC's president emailed me that we were just "a drug test and signature away" from getting started. It felt like all eyes were on me. I didn't want this job derailed by a debate over privacy rights. Nor did I want a reputation as someone who was picking fights with management even before his job started.

So with a medical attendant hovering nearby, I dutifully peed as directed.

Over the months, I was able to regain a little self-respect on the issue, by denouncing random drug testing in on-air debates. At my desk, I posted a bumper sticker given me by a *Donahue* producer: "The Only Urine Sample You'll Get from Me . . . Is for a Taste Test."

Mostly I stewed: If I had to take a drug test, why not MSNBC's big stars? Who among us hasn't wondered if *Hardball* motormouth Chris Matthews was hopped up on coke or something? And what about Alan Keyes? When I arrived at MSNBC, the flaming antigay crusader (with a lesbian daughter) was hosting the *Alan Keyes Is Making Sense* show. Don't tell me the executive who dreamt up that title could pass a drug test. *Slate* magazine offered an alternative title: *Alan Keyes Is Taking Meds.*

★  ★  ★

With my contract and drug test signed, sealed and excreted, I embarked on my first day at MSNBC headquarters in a converted warehouse in Secaucus, New Jersey—10 minutes across the Hudson River from Manhattan. It was a bizarre experience, which I might have attributed to drugs if a test had not just cleared me.

After picking up my employee badge from security, I ventured through the building's central corridor, where 10 framed posters celebrated the highlights of MSNBC's early history. The first one I saw: "The Funeral of Princess Diana, Sept. 6, 1997." Then: "Death of JFK Jr." On the opposite wall, I saw "Columbine Shootings, Live Coverage" and "Elian Gonzalez, Live Coverage" and "The Concorde Crash."

I'd spent years criticizing the tabloidization of mainstream news and TV's overcoverage and fetishizing of crashes and shootings. Here I was joining a channel that actually viewed these embarrassing episodes as high points worth boasting about. If these were MSNBC's highlights, what were its lowlights?

Thankfully, there was no poster "Monica's Dress, Round-the-Clock Coverage." MSNBC had devoted such nonstop coverage to Fellatiogate that I started referring to the channel in speeches and columns as "MSNBC: More Sex, Not by Chance." I'll never forget MSNBC's viewer poll in August 1998—"Clinton's morals: Should it be a political issue, or should it remain a private concern?" This was after the channel had spent seven months covering virtually nothing but "Clinton's morals."*

After passing through the Bizarro-world Hall of Fame corridor, my next stop was Human Resources—for orientation, filling out forms, choosing my benefits package. That's when I learned that a mandatory part of the orientation session was the viewing of a GE video on "integrity." It was the last straw. I protested.

"Look, I'm an expert on GE's felony status, its fraud convictions," I said to the HR staffer. "You're telling me I have to sit here and watch this video."

---

*It's easy to forget how essential cable news was in the drive to impeach Clinton for lying about sex. The Republican Right (driven by politics) and cable news (driven mostly by ratings over a sex story) operated as a tag team to keep the scandal at fever pitch. Quite a contrast to cable news' blasé reaction to Bush administration deception that led our nation to a devastating war four years later.

"Well, here's the video," he replied, probably fed up with me. "I'm not going to stand over you." He left the room. I watched the first minutes and shut it off.

## WORKIN' FOR THE MAN

When I was at FAIR, our magazine published a cover story about General Electric with the headline "Should Corporate Felons Own TV Stations?" In article after article, speech after speech, I questioned whether serious, independent journalism could survive at outlets owned by huge, politically active conglomerates. And now I was a journalist embedded deep inside the belly of the corporate media beast—working for a company that had done even more for Ronald Reagan's political career than Enron had for George W.'s.

Soon after GE took over NBC in 1986, CEO Jack Welch went up to the president of NBC News, poked him in the chest and shouted, "You work for GE!" That first day, I needed no reminder who my boss was. Nor could I forget all my previous criticism of GE, NBC and MSNBC. I knew I'd been hired largely to accommodate MSNBC's new star, Phil Donahue—but I wondered if the brass knew what I'd said about them. Or did they simply not care?

Ten months before I started working at MSNBC, I'd done a blistering interview with the Naderite magazine *Multinational Monitor* about GE's negative impact on journalism. I asked why the Federal Communications Commission allowed GE to get federal licenses to own TV stations: "If they deny broadcast licenses to individuals who had committed felonies in the past, why wouldn't that apply to corporate felons?"

In the interview, I listed incidents in which NBC staffers had censored or slanted the news out of deference to GE, and I discussed potential conflicts-of-interest—noting topics of journalistic inquiry in which GE has a direct interest: "taxes, trade, military spending, corporate welfare, sweatshops, the environment, etc."*

---

*In 1990, while researching a segment on consumer boycotts, an NBC *Today* show producer phoned boycott expert Todd Putnam and asked, "What's the biggest boycott going on right now?" When Putnam informed her that America's top boycott targeted GE over its production of nuclear weapons, she said, "We can't do that one. Well, we could do that one, but we won't." A number of weeks later, she told Putnam that *Today* was looking for a boycott that was "small," "local" and "sexy."

I spoke of my beloved Hudson River:

What producer from NBC, CNBC, MSNBC or even the History Channel (which GE owns a chunk of) would in their right mind produce a report on the Hudson River? . . . . The contamination of the Hudson River is a story that has everything. It has the visuals: people having to throw back the fish. It has the victims: these middle-class mom-and-pop fishing operations that have been totally wiped out. And it's got the villain: General Electric. . . . That's a dramatic story that could get a big audience, but you can't tell that story—not because it won't be sensational, but because it's too sensational.

I continued:

It explains why in 1998 MSNBC did the Monica Lewinsky story and the stained dress week after week after week. If the path to ratings that would include big news that affects middle-class people is blocked because of self-censorship or corporate structure, then that other path—celebrity fluff like the JFK crash, Jon-Benet, O.J., Princess Di or Monica Lewinsky—becomes the only acceptable path to ratings in corporate news. That's why we get so much of it, and as a result, people can identify where Monica Lewinsky got her dress but not their own member of Congress. And I would argue that General Electric likes that situation a lot.

I hadn't a clue when I said these words that MSNBC proudly commemorated its "celebrity fluff" coverage in its front corridor.

I'm well aware that *Multinational Monitor* is not a must-read among NBC or GE brass. But *Vanity Fair* is, especially when it publishes profiles of GE boss Jack Welch. Just months before my hiring, *Vanity Fair* quoted me hammering NBC yet again: "When it comes to GE, almost no one [at NBC] sticks his neck out. The Hudson River story is made

---

Still later, a more senior producer told Putnam that he feared for his job if GE were mentioned. When *Today* finally aired its segment, which included a live interview with Putnam, GE was never brought up. Nor was there room for a GE light bulb on the set alongside other boycotted products such as tuna, cigarettes and Nike sneakers. Not until Putnam left the studio and headed for the elevator did he meet an NBC employee eager to discuss GE. It wasn't a journalist. It was a janitor, who yelled, "So how is the boycott of GE going?"

for primetime; it has victims, visuals and a villain. It's because of who the villain is that *Dateline* hasn't gone to town on it."

★ ★ ★

A year before I moved to MSNBC, I'd blasted NBC president Bob Wright on *Fox News Watch*. It's worth noting that when GE put Wright in charge of NBC, he had virtually no journalism experience—his main experience at GE was in plastics.

ERIC BURNS: The federal government wants the General Electric corporation to pay half-a-billion dollars to clean up the Hudson River because of chemicals that GE dumped into the river legally over a 30-year period. Bob Wright—the president of NBC, which is owned by GE—is heading up a team of five lobbyists trying to persuade the New York City Council not to endorse the cleanup. And in case you don't know what might be wrong with that, Jeff Cohen.

COHEN: What signal does it send to NBC journalists when their boss is lobbying on one side of a controversy? The signal is: Don't cover the story or don't cover it independently. NBC is a division of GE that had nothing to do with contaminating the Hudson River. But NBC controls several TV networks and a local TV station.

BURNS: A major local station.

COHEN: Right. It's got everything to do with intimidating politicians who may go against the interests of GE, NBC's corporate parent. This was insidious.

BURNS: I think what we should do here, Jim, is acknowledge the fact that all networks are owned by individuals who have vested interests that they want to see protected and that may be bad for journalism. It's just that this seems to be a more blatant case of showing it.

JIM PINKERTON. Right. You can't blame General Electric for having a position on the PCB issue. But you can blame Bob Wright, the president of a network, doing it. Once a year [big smile], Jeff is right.

★  ★  ★

After switching off the GE "integrity" video, I reentered the Hall of Shame en route to a meeting with MSNBC president Erik Sorenson. He had a modest office next to the sprawling, high-tech central studios with rotating anchor desks and assorted gadgetry. (Too bad viewers weren't equipped with ejector buttons for those anchor desks.)

TV news executives typically seem more like centrist politicians than journalists (not counting the rightwing politicians at Fox). Sorenson was no exception. He was a smart, skilled, glib politician—a likeable and diplomatic guy in an impossible job who, despite his work-related stresses, could easily have won a Mr. Congeniality award.

I've met many of the best journalists in our country. None are politician-like.

Sorenson was the channel's president, but decisions had to be negotiated with a bulky leadership group that included the president of NBC News and the former GE Plastics guy who ran NBC. MSNBC's Politburo made one bad decision after another, shifted its schedule constantly and remained mired in last place among the cable news channels—with no individual held responsible for the bad decisions.

At my meeting with Sorenson, he gently informed me that my promised job co-hosting a daily show had evaporated. All I would get would be a (roughly 10-minute) debate each afternoon with a right-winger to be determined each day and some substitute co-hosting. My first day at work and my on-camera role was shrinking. It wasn't a good omen.

MSNBC soon announced two new debate shows for its afternoon lineup. One would be hosted by Pat Buchanan and Bill Press, who'd become friends while anchoring CNN's *Crossfire*. The other would be hosted by Guardian Angels founder Curtis Sliwa and attorney Ron Kuby, bringing their revved-up *Curtis & Kuby* radio show to cable news.

I would end up getting plenty of co-hosting duties as a substitute for Kuby. The leftwing lawyer, it turns out, was an ardent "family values" dad whose contract called for him to have three-day weekends all summer with his family.

★   ★   ★

In May 2002, a week after orientation, my MSNBC job began . . . at full gallop. While it would take months of planning and haggling to launch *Donahue*, I started appearing immediately in daily debates with conservative pundits. Early topics included post-9/11 restrictions on civil liberties and FBI/CIA ineptitude in failing to prevent the attacks. I sent out a mass email to friends letting them know of my MSNBC gig:

> It's a bit ironic that I now appear on a news channel owned jointly by GE and Microsoft. But so far, so good. The other day, I declared that "the CIA seems better at overthrowing democratic governments than at tracking Al Qaeda terrorists." I quipped that we might one day be calling the FBI director *J. Edgar Mueller* and days later it was the headline of a *N.Y. Times* op-ed.

I received many emails in response. An old friend who'd become a successful politician in California joked that I'd "sold out" to corporate media. A friend at CNN sent these words of . . . well . . . discouragement: "From one employee of one reprehensible media conglomerate to another, good luck."

My favorite email came from Noam Chomsky. The MIT linguist and U.S. foreign policy critic wrote, "Jeff: Sounds great. Almost enough to convince me to get cable access—but not quite."

Did he know something I didn't?

## IN SEARCH OF "THE LIBERAL MEDIA"

I admit it. As soon as I arrived at MSNBC headquarters in Secaucus, I went off in search of "The Liberal Media" among the hundreds of media professionals working there. After Fox News, it was refreshing to be at a more mainstream outlet run by NBC News, the top news division in American television. A network like MSNBC was supposed to be infested with liberals pushing their agendas and spinning the news. Given my long workdays, if they were there, it wouldn't be hard for us to meet up. But I couldn't find them.

So I kept looking . . . and looking. Eventually I found about seven of them—including makeup artists, camera operators, archivists and interns.

John Moody at Fox had complained about the Sandinista-lovers in the mainstream media. I had trouble finding folks who knew who the Sandinistas were.

I couldn't find traces of "The Liberal Media" even in the MSNBC parking lot, where hundreds of employees parked their cars. The one candidate bumper sticker I ever saw was for the Republican running for Maryland governor. The only war-related one I saw was a hawkish American flag sticker: "These Colors Don't Run." (After the word "Run," I felt like penciling in ". . . the World.") And there was one that still baffles me: "Chicks Dig Bumper Stickers."

The only progressive bumper sticker in the whole lot was the one on my car—a FAIR sticker that illuminated the irony of my presence there: "Don't Trust the Corporate Media."

★ ★ ★

Soon after starting at MSNBC, I had an odd exchange with my daughter Cady, then 5 years old.

CADY: Daddy, what does your bumper sticker say?

DAD: It says, "Don't Trust the Corporate Media."

CADY [puzzled expression on her face]: But aren't you the media?

DAD: I'm just a small part of it, honey. You can trust me.

★ ★ ★

I couldn't find liberalism at MSNBC, but I did find a strict corporate hierarchy. At the bottom were bookers and associate producers—energetic, upbeat and powerless. In the middle were producers who'd learned how not to rock boats, dispirited over constantly shifting instructions from above, often hanging on to jobs they were quite cynical about. There weren't many budding Seymour

Hershes in that stratum. Near the top were executive producers and on-air "talent"—privileged folks who'd forgotten (or never learned) what aggressive journalism was; their main job, aided by their agents, seemed to be staying cozy with management.

MSNBC management was afraid of its own shadow—adept at placating bosses at GE/NBC and powerbrokers in Washington, and terrified about independent journalism that might offend someone important. These were imitators, not initiators. And Fox News was the industry leader.

The final power was in the owner's hands—which meant that the shots were called ultimately by GE and the GE Plastics guy who ran NBC.

In TV news, executives and "talent" are so overpaid that their elite status tends to chill any impulse toward controversy or challenging authority. I saw up close how easy it is to get addicted to salaries of $200,000 or more, fine homes, luxury cars, private schools—and how unthinkable to rock corporate boats over journalistic principle. I found no label sillier than "talent." At least the techies and video editors had actual skills; "talent" are mostly teeth-and-hair talking heads bound by conventional wisdom, or rip-and-read pundits bound by partisan scripts.

Having come to MSNBC from Fox in 2002, the difference in troop morale was palpable. While Fox initially felt like a college TV station, it soon developed a confident swagger as it found its audience. Fox had direction: rightward. MSNBC had direction, too: zig-zag. Low ratings and ever-changing orders had left the grunts shell-shocked and deflated; MSNBC was filthy with gossip and backbiting.

I was in MSNBC's newsroom in October 2002 when GE's new CEO, Jeff Immelt, went on Fox News and praised Fox as "the industry standard"—declaring that he wanted MSNBC to be as "interesting and as edgy as you guys are." Not exactly a morale booster.

★ ★ ★

I'd been a GE employee a few months when the messy divorce of Jack Welch, GE's recently retired CEO, spilled into the newspapers. The court filings of the jilted Mrs. Welch indicated that Mr. Welch's retirement perks—besides his $750,000 monthly pension check—included free use of GE jets, helicopters and a limited-edition Mercedes; courtside seats at sporting events around the world; membership fees at five country clubs; and a $15 million company condo on Central Park

West with staff, lavish food and wine provisions, dry cleaning, toiletries and flowers.

I found the revelations to be stunning, and I imagined how many top-notch journalists could have been hired with those resources if GE and NBC were as committed to serious journalism as to pampering its former CEO.

My anger wasn't shared by everyone at MSNBC. A high-level producer commented, "I don't care what perks Jack Welch gets, as long as he keeps the GE stock price up." I couldn't picture this journalist battling to expose corporate greed or chicanery—let alone recognizing the harm it causes to workaday Americans.

Months later, after GE raised health insurance premiums and co-pays on its employees and retirees, nearly 20,000 unionized GE workers staged a nationwide protest strike. A picketer in Kentucky was hit by a police car and killed. MSNBC is virtually union-free (as are Fox News and CNN), but I felt the need to do something in the name of free speech and solidarity. So I placed United Electrical Workers fliers in the bathrooms of MSNBC. Later, I saw that a co-worker had moved my leaflets into the official notice frames where one could read them while standing at the urinals.

The union leaflet noted that "GE is getting set to announce record profits of over $15 billion for 2002" and that the healthcare changes "will amount to about a $30 million transfer to GE this year from employees and retirees. That's about the value of the various retirement homes that the Company has provided to Jack Welch."

## STAGE LEFT

While I never got to co-host my own MSNBC show each day, I did get a regular slot for serious debates every afternoon with an opponent chosen from a roster of conservative gabbers. I thought of it as my show, even though it ran only 10 minutes—and shrunk to five minutes by the end.

On opening day, my debating foe was Armstrong Williams, who would soon gain fame as a buckraker rather than a muckraker. (More on that later.) I came out of my corner aggressively demanding a full investigation of the "intelligence blunders that led to Sept. 11," including the "CIA's work in Afghanistan that gave birth to Al Qaeda." Jabbing

Muckracker vs. Buckraker

at Williams, I called for a probe "of why the CIA in the 1980s, under your friend Ronald Reagan, was scouring the Islamic world recruiting extremists, arming them, training them in Afghanistan against a Soviet Union that was falling apart." His response was nonsubstantive: "Jeff, you're too intelligent for this."

A management favorite was Jack Burkman, a square-jawed and block-headed Republican strategist who joined me to argue about how our country should treat detainees arrested in the "war on terror"—a war we were told would never end. Debates with the pugnacious Burkman generated little light but "lots of energy." MSNBC once identified him as a "trial attorney," but I never in my life encountered an attorney who had less use for trials.

Not all my debates were the high-voltage ones cherished in cable news. I remember a real dud—in other words, a smart and sober discussion—with Republican congressman Bob Barr. It wasn't clear until we went on the air that this rightwing former FBI agent had the same privacy concerns about FBI anti-terrorism strategies as I, a leftwing ACLUer.

One of my preferred debating partners was the youthful editor of the *National Review*, Rich Lowry, a bit more cerebral than your typical conservative pundit (another high jump over a low hurdle). During one debate, I hoped to confound Lowry by proposing a shake-up in the names of federal departments:

> Department of Homeland Security sounds Orwellian to me. Since they want to put all these security and defense agencies in one department, why not call that the Department of Defense—and have what's currently called the Department of Defense go back to its name in 1947: the Department of War. Those titles would be more descriptive, more accurate. What would be wrong with that, Rich?

Lowry confounded me by responding: "That makes total sense." It was his position, too, and that of his magazine.

Day after day at MSNBC, I tried to broaden the discourse on cable news by advocating positions not usually heard: for treating drug abuse medically and not criminally; for following the lead of Western European countries (as opposed to Saudi Arabia, Iran and China) by abolishing the death penalty; for an evenhanded Middle East policy that promoted a genuine Palestinian state and an end to Israeli occupation and settlement of Palestinian territories.

I argued repeatedly that the 9/11 attacks could have been prevented—without loosening surveillance guidelines—if the Bush team had been more focused on Al Qaeda and less so on California pot smokers or New Orleans prostitutes. I continuously blasted Bush administration efforts to subvert a thorough investigation of 9/11.

I criticized the Democratic Party for being "an opposition party afraid to oppose" Bush extremism—especially Democrat leaders Tom Daschle and Dick Gephardt: "They are a case study in political and parliamentary incompetence." (It's easy to forget that Democrats controlled the Senate in 2002.)

My favorite issue, one that placed me in the role of advocate for the middle class, was the corporate crime spree (Enron, WorldCom, et al.) then being exposed. I blamed it on 20 years of deregulation and corruption in Washington, made worse by a Bush administration that was "ideologically opposed to having cops on the corporate beat" (unless they were energy regulators chosen by Enron)—and was obstructing "commonsense regulation" that would protect workers, retirees and small investors. I repeatedly noted "Enron's central role in the rise of George Bush's political career" and pounded the GOP for letting businesses "take a Bermuda address and thereby evade taxes."

Overpaid TV talking heads are not known for railing against economic inequality. I was an exception, pointing out that "the average CEO of a major corporation is paid more than $10 million a year. Twenty years ago, CEOs earned about 40 times that of the average hourly employee; now it's 500 times that of the hourly employee."

On the issue that came to dominate my tenure at MSNBC—Bush's relentless push for war in Iraq—I gave the antiwar movement a regular voice on cable news. My opposition was emphatic and prescient about the bloody mess that would follow a U.S. invasion. I imputed partisan political motives to Bush's war drive and its timing. I said the war would play into the hands of Al Qaeda–type jihadists. While Bushites said that invading Iraq would be a "cake walk," I warned of a "quagmire"—"a massive war" that would be "much bigger and much more costly than the last Gulf War."*

I never lost sight of the fact that I wouldn't have been on MSNBC spouting off like this if not for my bond with Phil Donahue. It was obvious that my views made some at the channel uncomfortable. My afternoon debates were moderated by "objective" news anchors—one of whom went out of his way week after week to distance himself from the views of the network's lefty pundit. At Fox News, I might have suspected that he'd received a memo from Moody. At MSNBC, there was probably a simpler explanation—the dread of appearing "liberal."

I couldn't discuss the weather at MSNBC unless balanced by a hardcore rightist. As the Iraq war approached, I appeared on-air less and less—supplanted by "military analysts" and "weapons experts" who required neither balance nor tough questions from the anchors.

## FALWELL, COULTER & ME

One afternoon, in a flashback to my Fox days, I was asked to debate not one but two rightwingers: Rich Lowry and reputed Moral Majority leader Jerry Falwell. You'll remember that days after 9/11, Rev. Falwell had blamed the attacks on "the feminists and the gays . . . the ACLU, People for the American Way" and other secularizers who'd provoked God's wrath against America. Later, he contributed to ecumenical tolerance the world over by calling the Prophet Mohammed "a terrorist."

Our debate topic was separation of church and state. Jolly ol' Falwell seemed in love with his own voice as he preached his gospel: "Much of public education today," he intoned, "is designed to create an atheistic society that totally repudiates our religious heritage. This

---

* Two weeks into the invasion, with U.S. troops encircling Baghdad, I wrote a widely circulated column for CommonDreams.org warning of the future: "After the U.S. 'wins' the war, will Iraq become the new West Bank—with suicide bombers and snipers targeting U.S. soldiers occupying another parcel of Arab land? Will U.S. soldiers have to set up an Israeli-style roadblock and checkpoint system, and search vehicles, backpacks, even handbags to protect themselves and any U.S.-installed Iraqi regime? After the U.S. military replaces Saddam Hussein's secular national dictatorship, will the mantle of opposition in Iraq and beyond pass to the more dangerous, transnational Islamist terrorists?"

is a nation under God!" Lowry chuckled approvingly as the reverend attacked a federal judge— married to the head of the Southern California ACLU (my former boss)—as "to the left of Gorbachev."

Near the end of the debate, I reiterated a point I'd opened with that had gone unanswered: "Rev. Falwell, if we are a nation under God, it's interesting that the founders of our Constitution, our framers, didn't even put the word [God] in the Constitution. That was by design."

"You haven't read it very clearly," Falwell responded. "Let me correct you on that. The Constitution is dated 1787 in the year - of - our - *Lord*."

He slowed down to enunciate each precious word, considering it a "gotcha" moment. Falwell and I were on a split screen: As he sternly pointed his finger at me, I shook my head, face in my hands, in disbelief.

Laughing again, Lowry crowed, "Reverend, don't say that word. You're making Jeff very nervous."

I felt caught in the middle of an on-air exorcism.

The debate closed with Falwell continuing to a big finale: "The separation of church and state is a myth," declared the preacher, "like global warming."

All three of us were now on split-screen: Lowry had gone glum. I was laughing at the ignorance I'd just heard. And Falwell appeared very self-satisfied over his pro-God/anti-environment twofer.*

---

*It wasn't until I'd scrutinized the tape (with the diligence some study the Zapruder film) that I realized that Falwell was still sermonizing at the end, as the anchor thanked his guests—something about there being no way to heaven "except through Christ."

★ ★ ★

In my regular timeslot in June 2002, I was set to debate Ann Coulter, who was on tour promoting a book called *Slander*. Coulter was firmly established as the top shock jock of cable news—or, in the words of a *Boston Globe* columnist, a "rightwing telebimbo." I knew from hanging out with too many conservative pundits in too many greenrooms that her TV stardom was the source of envy; they groused that she used her legs, miniskirts and sleek blond hair to gain unfair advantage over other rightwing yakkers. I heard this complaint mostly from men over 50.

I'm willing to believe Coulter when she publicly proclaims that she is not anorexic or bulimic. But I did wonder if her unfair advantage was some sort of diet/pep pill. Not that drugs would excuse her of personal responsibility for muddle-brained comments—like referring to Tipper Gore as "gaudy white trash." Or talking about "the benefits of local fascism." Or calling for public flogging of juveniles, because it wouldn't be cool "in the 'hood" to be flogged.

I wondered if she was sober in 1997 when, as an MSNBC contributor, she debated Vietnam veteran Bobby Muller about landmines. Discussing Vietnam, Muller said, "In 90 percent of cases that U.S. soldiers got blown up—Ann, are you listening?—they were our own mines." At which point Coulter interrupted to say. "No wonder you guys lost." She said that to a man who took a bullet in Vietnam, leaving him paralyzed from the chest down.

I suspect that the happy-pill hypothesis persists because, as cable news viewers know all too well, Coulter is so often laughing inappropriately while spouting her odious commentary.

To me, Coulter is something of a cross between Joan Rivers and Eva Braun. Now I have a general rule against Eva Braun comparisons, ever since my pal Randy Credico, a comedian, got banned from the *Tonight Show* 20 years ago—after he quipped that whenever he saw America's UN ambassador Jean Kirkpatrick on TV, he had to wonder "if Eva Braun really died in that bunker in 1945." I've made an exception in Coulter's case. (It's worth noting that in

*Slander*, she called Katie Couric "the affable Eva Braun of morning television.")

I looked forward to my Coulter debate, which had been scheduled a week in advance. I read chunks of *Slander* (for which I deserved combat pay) and prepared questions. But I wasn't totally sure whether the book was serious or self-parody. Its thesis is that liberals engage in name-calling because they can't engage in logical, factual debate. This from an author who doesn't limit her insults to Democrats like Hillary "Pond Scum" Clinton; she called the Republican EPA chief Christie Todd Whitman a "bird brain" and former GOP senator Jim Jeffords a "half-wit." When the rightwing editors of *National Review* rejected a Coulter column urging enhanced airport vigilance against "suspicious-looking swarthy males," she called the editors "girly-boys."

On page 2 of her book, I learned that liberals have "a hatred of Christians"—and, a few pages later, that "liberals hate America" and "hate all religions except Islam." On page 5, I read, "*New York Times* columnist Frank Rich demanded that [Attorney General] Ashcroft stop monkeying around with Muslim terrorists and concentrate on anti-abortion extremists." This claim was sheer invention and offered almost a textbook example of slander, the apparently un-ironic title of her book.

With my questions ready, I got into makeup, put in my earpiece and headed to the set as I did around that time each day. But just before airtime, my producer informed me, "She won't debate you."

I was incredulous: "This was set a long time ago. I'm ready to go."

"She's not," replied the producer. "She claims she knew nothing about a debate."

I was a network staffer ready to debate the contents of a book. The author was a guest, unwilling to debate. Which one of us do you think went on the air? Ann Coulter, of course—appearing with an anchor ill-prepared to ask tough questions.

If MSNBC were following the codes of journalism, an author unwilling to debate her controversial book would not be given a free ride. But MSNBC follows the codes of conformity and show biz: Coulter is a draw, so she dictates the terms of debate . . . or nondebate.

So much for "The Liberal Media."

Page 1 of Coulter's book refers to "the left's hegemonic control of the news media." The more she and her brethren bluster about bias, the more they dominate a corporate media system only too happy to oblige them.

# CHAPTER SIX
## INSIDE THE SAUSAGE FACTORY

The process of journalism is often compared to sausage-making—an ugly and unappetizing process that is best unseen by those who hope to enjoy its consumption. As a media critic, I'd long known that the end product of TV journalism was often unhealthy, even toxic. Now that I was inside the sausage factory, working 10-hour days in MSNBC's newsroom, I could see the day-to-day orders, priorities and rules that led to the product turning out like it did.

Since I was an outsider, newsroom codes and rituals that others took for granted struck me as quite peculiar. When I asked why certain practices were in place, I would sometimes get blank stares. Or staffers would be too busy to stop doing what they were doing to explain to me why they were doing it. The sausage factory, to butcher my slaughterhouse metaphor, seemed to be inhabited by chickens without heads.

To figure out why the factory line operated as it did, I couldn't rely just on the factory workers or the foremen. The production plan was determined by executives beyond the factory floor—who made their decisions based on reading (or misreading) the viewing habits of their audience, with one eye on their owners' interests and another on the needs of their paying customers: the sponsors.

★ ★ ★

One of the first things I noticed in MSNBC's newsroom: No one listens. The visual is everything. On every producer's desk, TV sets were usually tuned to MSNBC . . . but virtually no one paid attention to the substance of what we were transmitting. I fantasized about interrupting one of my debates to announce that U.S. troops had invaded

France—just to see if any of the overworked, deadlined producers would notice.

As soon as I'd finish a live debate in the central studio, I'd return to my desk alongside a dozen co-workers and look for feedback: "How'd I do? Did I make sense?" One after another would tell me, "I didn't hear it, but you looked real good." Or, "It looked great—lots of energy!" After embarrassingly overheated on-air confrontations—fingers pointing, head shaking, eyes rolling—I'd receive thumbs-up gestures and "great energy!" verdicts from colleagues who hadn't a clue what I'd said.

In cable news, management covets "energy"—a euphemism for shouting, or sufficient friction or fervor to keep viewers from changing channels. Generating heat is far more important than shedding light. "Good energy" means "good theater." In the phrase "news show," the operative word is *show*.

It didn't take me long to pick up newsroom lingo. A guest booking is a "get." It's a "great get" if you book a hugely famous guest—or a timely one, like the mother of a recently kidnapped child, or a teenager whose foot was just chewed off by a shark. When trying to locate and book a guest, you are "efforting" him or her. In the Adam Sandler movie *Mr. Deeds*, a tabloid TV news producer played by Winona Ryder is efforting potential guests who knew a recently deceased tycoon. But she can find no one closer to the tycoon than his barber. *Not* a great "get." "The freaking barber! That's the best you could get me?" growls the boss in horror.

## IF IT SCARES, IT BLARES

One newsroom rule I repeatedly ran up against was the one favoring live "breaking news." It led to several last-minute cancellations of my debate segments. A week before I was bumped from the Ann Coulter segment by Ann Coulter, I was scheduled to appear with Congressman Bob Barr. But an exciting car chase in California intervened. A few days after that, my segment was nixed because of "developments" (which turned out to be utterly insignificant) in a child kidnapping case in Utah.

The live event rules cable news, especially in daytime. In the blink of an eye, scheduled programming is cancelled for something, anything, "live"—perhaps a police chief announcing news in a child kidnapping case. Or announcing there is no news in a kidnapping case.

Or that there'd been no kidnapping after all and the child had been with a neighbor.

During my tenure at MSNBC, cable news was obsessed with several horrific cases of girls abducted by strangers from inside or near their homes—such as Danielle van Dam of San Diego, Elizabeth Smart of Salt Lake City and Samantha Runnion of Orange County. Abductions were especially "newsworthy" if the victim was white—preferably blond—and upper middle-class. (The case of Alexis Patterson, a 7-year-old black girl who vanished in Milwaukee during this period, was somehow not very newsworthy.)

Don't get me wrong. As the father of two young girls, I know these stories can be riveting, can prod parents to greater security, and in some cases can even thwart a crime or bring a perpetrator to justice. But what spurs the inflamed cable coverage is usually just ratings. Otherwise, we'd see the fate of more minority victims on screen. Prior to 24-hour cable news, child abductions were local stories. Dramatic, scary . . . and local. "New media" like all-news cable were supposed to shrink the globe by making world events local. But with "news" in the hands of the entertainment conglomerates, the opposite was happening, too: local stories were going global.

Kidnap coverage was so extensive in 2002 that viewers could not be faulted for believing that our country was in the grip of an epidemic. Yet statistics showed no increase in child kidnappings—it was only TV coverage of abductions, thanks to cable news, that was booming. "Last year, it was shark attacks," a criminologist told *USA Today* in July. "This year, it's child abductions. People see a couple of cases that cluster together in time, and they think there's an epidemic. There's not."

Summer 2001 had indeed been the summer of shark attacks, at least on cable news. Only Gary Condit had topped the sharks. Another epidemic? Shark attacks in the United States did go up that year—from 54 to 55—but fell worldwide.

Whether shark attacks or street crime or terror alerts, TV news has always relied on fear to capture an audience—a reality exposed vividly in Michael Moore's *Bowling for Columbine*. In the cavalcade of crime, car chases and fires known as local TV news, the motto is "If it bleeds, it leads." On cable news, our motto could have been "If it scares, it blares." And "If it terrifies, no need to verify."

As a guest on *Donahue* in August 2002, I criticized the compulsive coverage of child abductions:

The media are supposed to be the watchdogs for society, warning us against real dangers and real problems. But because of the for-profit nature of the media—competitive, 24/7, the search for ratings—we have a watchdog that's always barking. Now watchdogs cannot be real useful unless they bark when there's a danger and quit barking when there's no danger.

★ ★ ★

In October 2002, cable news was seized by a suspense thriller of chilling proportions: "The Beltway Sniper." Over a period of weeks, 10 people were killed and three seriously wounded in random rifle attacks from long range in and around Washington, D.C. Ambush shootings occurred at gas stations and parking lots outside schools, restaurants and supermarkets. It was a genuine story; initially, there were even fears it was linked to Al Qaeda. I was an MSNBC talking head during the news miniseries, which was propelled by hours of speculation from pundits, law enforcement experts and "profilers." Most of our predictions about the gunman—who, how, why, even how many (it turned out to be a duo)—were wrong. Ratings were super, though.

★ ★ ★

One afternoon at MSNBC, I watched our channel and others breathlessly follow a sketchy but frightening story that vials of a deadly bacteria (smallpox or bubonic plague) had been stolen from a lab. With little information available, tension mounted as MSNBC vowed to stay on top of the breaking story; the onscreen banner read something like "Smallpox Vials Stolen?" Near the beginning, I warned co-workers that the whole story smelled fishy. In due time, there was a live news conference at which a local law enforcement official said they had no evidence that anything had been stolen but that vials were unaccounted for. Even after he'd made the point a couple times, the word *stolen* remained in MSNBC's lower-third banner. I had to practically run into the control room before the banner was changed.

A short time later came the announcement that the vials had been located. Nothing was stolen; nothing was missing. The story disappeared faster than you could say "Gary Condit," never to be mentioned again on MSNBC or anywhere else—with no explanation or apology offered.

Factual mistakes will be made in any journalistic endeavor. What I saw in cable news was that errors and sloppiness were not just occasional. Nor were they random. The sloppiness with facts typically went in the same direction—tending to exaggerate the story. This was born of the need to "go live," to speculate, to hold an audience.

★   ★   ★

I often wondered about the calculations of cable news management. Car chases and kidnappings and missing vials can pump up ratings in the short term. But what hope did such fare offer for long-term viewership? How long before the thrill of "breaking" news wears off? And if such stories are enough to temporarily interest certain viewers, aren't they the ones most likely to migrate away from cable "news" to the dozens of entertainment channels?

In the wake of round-the-clock coverage of Princess Diana's death, MSNBC was ridiculed by none other than Fox's Roger Ailes, who told *USA Today*, "MSNBC is under such pressure to get ratings, they've gone totally tabloid." Let's be clear: Fox News can go "totally tabloid" as well as anyone—but its rightwing agenda sometimes provides a push toward politics and policy news that MSNBC lacks. That agenda built Fox's core audience.

MSNBC execs never seemed to question whether tabloid-style news, essentially entertainment programming, can sustain an audience when there are better entertainment choices out there.

## PRODUCED BY . . . KARL ROVE

Schooled in the protocols of cable news, the Bush administration brilliantly exploited its worship of live events. At MSNBC, I witnessed producers nearly orgasm at word that the White House would soon be serving up a photo-op or briefing. Upon hearing of these events—called "pressers"—all else is put on hold to assure that the second the administration event starts, MSNBC and the other news channels are ready to air it live.

In 2002, the Bush team might schedule a White House press secretary's briefing ("the president stands tough against terrorism") . . . often followed by a Pentagon briefing ("war on terror is on track") . . . often followed by an afternoon speech from President Bush in front of a patriotic flag backdrop and cheering handpicked crowd . . . perhaps followed by a briefing on the latest terrorism arrest or scare from the Justice Department or Homeland Security. Through its ability to dictate the rhythms of the news day, the White House's often singular view of reality would air at length in near monologue fashion.

Such dominance of the media agenda bred contempt at the White House for facts and journalism. In a conversation with author Ron Suskind during this period, an anonymous senior Bush adviser dismissed journalists and others of "the reality-based community"—explaining, "We're an empire now, and when we act, we create our own reality. And while you're studying that reality . . . we'll act again, creating other new realities."

**YOU WRITE WHAT YOU'RE TOLD!**

THANKS, CORPORATE NEWS!
We Couldn't Control The People Without You
A Message From The Ministry Of Homeland Security

For a country to be reality-based and democratic, journalism must give officials a reality check—not a blank check. On cable news, the Bush administration used its staggered schedule of daily events and speeches—with little challenge from journalists—to stoke fear throughout 2002 about terrorism and Iraq, and to promote its deceptive domestic agenda. As I sat at my MSNBC desk watching Bush or a top associate carry on, I knew painfully well that my network would not be following the administration event with a critical view, no matter how dubious or manipulative were the official claims. To do so—to practice actual journalism—might prompt the dreaded charge of "liberal bias."

And actual journalism might undermine the "show." Stars might refuse to appear on your channel. Big "gets" from the White House would be found only on rival programs.

Three weeks after the 9/11 attacks, I appeared with mainstream journalists on a panel at American University, where I remarked that the star guests dominating news coverage were former secretaries of state and defense who were never "asked the obvious questions" about their own failures that led us to Sept. 11. Ray Suarez from PBS's *NewsHour* agreed that these eminent figures "are being used as expert guests with very little reference to their actual past as policymakers." Suarez then faced a question from the panel's moderator, Professor Jane Hall (my colleague on *Fox News Watch*).

HALL: So you have one of these people coming on your show, they're a "good get" as we call it in TV show parlance. How are you going to look to your viewers, first of all, if you go after them . . . and will you get them back a second time?

SUAREZ: Access is like oxygen when you're a reporter. And if you're going to do something, I guess, that's going to jeopardize access in the future, you better be pretty sure that this person who is going to perceive what you are about to do to them as burning them is someone who you can do without in the future after you burn them.

In an environment where political figures are treated as Hollywood royalty, with access to them being paramount, asking a difficult or unwelcome question is seen as "burning" them.

When Phil Donahue toughly interviewed big-name guests, MSNBC management was petrified that the VIPs would be offended and not make return engagements. "Access is everything in Washington," Phil later told a reporter. "If you're the executive producer at one of the big news shows and you piss off Karl Rove, you're not going to get Condi or Rummy or any of those guests who would legitimize your show as a serious, important program."

★ ★ ★

By the spring of 2002, the pro-Bush tilt on cable news was so pronounced that even the dozy Democratic leaders in Congress were moved to protest. In a letter to the heads of CNN, Fox and MSNBC, they complained that the dominance of live White House events (even on domestic issues) "muffles" Democrats and "undercuts the debate that is the heart of our democracy." CNN carried 157 live administration events vs. only seven from the Democrats in the first months of 2002.

But the bias favoring Bush events—whether newsworthy or just made-for-TV rallies produced by Karl Rove—only worsened as Bush started pushing for war with Iraq. The country was evenly divided on the war; TV news coverage was not. And the bias continued right through the 2002 congressional election, when one might have expected CNN and MSNBC (forget Fox) to have cared at least about the pretense of balance.

Molly Ivins pointed to television coverage as a "major factor" in the last-minute upsurge that led Republicans to electoral victory: "Almost the only political story for the last three days was Bush Barnstorming.

It's as though reporters were covering a presidential campaign with only one candidate rather than a midterm election."

## FEAR AND FEVER IN THE NEWSROOM

Inside the sausage factory, the protocols of cable news are easy to learn. Scary is good. Scary and live is better. Scary and live with powerful footage is best of all. It's the trifecta. When my debate on a serious issue with a controversial member of Congress ran up against a car chase yielding dramatic live footage, I knew my segment didn't stand a chance.

TV news is a visual medium, where exciting video is sacred. Over the years, I've heard many a TV producer sermonize about the need for gripping video. Car chase footage is revered—it may end as crash footage (and edited crash footage can do well in reruns).

But rules have their exceptions, and every sausage factory grunt learns these as well. . . .

There is one type of compelling video that is off-limits in U.S. television: war footage. Especially footage of civilian victims of U.S. military action. War may be the most unreal of all the unrealities on TV news. The invasion of Iraq was just another TV show, with triumphant music and graphics added—dramatic enhancements that would be silly and superfluous if the guts of the story had not been totally excised. War footage is flash and boom and, at worst, scared soldiers scurrying about—but the actual point of war, killing and maiming, is almost never shown.

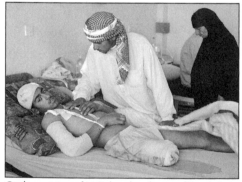
Civilian victim of U.S. bombardment of Baghdad

In Iraq and Afghanistan, tens of thousands of civilians have been killed or seriously wounded by the most horrific weapons ever assembled by a single army—ours. But we rarely catch a glimpse of these victims. Unless we watch foreign newscasts, we're blissfully ignorant of the ghastly reality seen by the rest of the world.

When U.S. forces invaded Afghanistan in October 2001, CNN executives sent memos instructing their staff to balance any image of civilian Afghan casualties with commentary reminding viewers that "the Taliban regime in Afghanistan continues to harbor terrorists." Even though "it may start sounding rote," one memo demanded that anchors keep repeating that "U.S. military actions are in response to a terrorist attack that killed close to 5,000 innocent people." This was weeks after 9/11. Who'd forgotten?

CNN execs were insistent on downplaying the suffering of innocent Afghan civilians—many of whom were women—due to the actions of the tyrannical Taliban that had been oppressing them. (Imagine how we'd react if a foreign news network wouldn't show images of American 9/11 victims without "balancing" commentary reminding viewers of some U.S. government atrocity.)

After the memos leaked, CNN chair Walter Isaacson—who authored one of them—told the *Washington Post* that it "seems perverse to focus too much on the casualties or hardship in Afghanistan."

One of the most potent biases imparted by U.S. media is that the lives of Americans matter more than the lives of others, especially those with dark skin hues. Some call this bias "ethnocentrism"—an unnecessarily fancy word for racism.

★ ★ ★

I was at MSNBC in 2002 when polls started showing that most Americans did not know who had attacked us the previous Sept. 11. It's hard to imagine a more devastating indictment of today's media. What event had received more coverage than 9/11? Yet most of the public wrongly believed that Iraq's Saddam Hussein had been "personally involved" in the attacks—by a margin of 53 to 34 percent, in an August Gallup poll. Weeks before the Iraq war, a CNN/*Time* poll found that 72 percent believed Saddam's involvement in 9/11 was somewhat or very likely.

A misunderstanding of that nature and proportion isn't transmitted by relatives at a family gathering or neighbors across a picket fence. It's transmitted by the media. Serious news consumers knew that the culprit was Al Qaeda and that Al Qaeda and Saddam were adversaries. But most Americans aren't serious news consumers; they may be immersed in media 10 hours a day, but it's mostly entertainment media—with just enough news or news headlines to be confused or manipulated.

Much of the misunderstanding can be credited to the Bush forces. They deliberately sowed confusion about 9/11 as their enemy morphed from Bin Laden into Saddam and they repeatedly linked, without serious evidence, Al Qaeda to Iraq's dictator. But White House spin would have failed to mislead if major media like cable news had diligently challenged inaccurate claims from Bush spokespersons—*even at the risk of being accused of liberal bias.* MSNBC management would have had to decide that journalism is more than running cameras at every live Bush event and that each covered event required serious analysis of falsehoods and innuendo coming from the Bush team.*

MSNBC's coverage sometimes confused rather than clarified the reality that Saddam and Al Qaeda were two distinct forces. Like tabloid newspapers, cable news relies on banner headlines; MSNBC's main banner for months leading up to the Iraq war was "Showdown with Saddam." It was ubiquitous, even when misleading. At a briefing in early 2003, Homeland Security chief Tom Ridge discussed precautions against Al Qaeda–type terrorism. The briefing had nothing to do with Saddam. Yet during parts of the live event, MSNBC's banner read, "Showdown with Saddam."

At Fox News during this period, confusion about 9/11 was bred by an ideological imperative to help Bush make his case for war with Iraq. While some news outlets debated whether invading Iraq would help or hinder the fight against Al Qaeda terrorists, Fox had decided

THe iNFORMaTiON AGe

the issue for its viewers; when a possible invasion of Iraq was discussed, its banner was "War on Terror."

Whether media ineptitude or fear or ideology was at work, the reality is stark: America made war against a country that had not attacked us on 9/11—with much of America believing that it had.

---

*Saddam-9/11 confusion among casual TV viewers was also generated by pre–Iraq war debates that followed a standard script. Dove (soberly): "Why rush to war when there are alternatives?" Hawk (fervently): "Have you forgotten that 3,000 people have died!"

★  ★  ★

One newsroom fear is rarely discussed but increasingly present as bigger and bigger companies take over the media: the dread of covering the boss's business. The multinationals that own TV news—like General Electric, Time Warner, Disney and News Corporation—have significant political, economic and environmental impacts; they have big lobbying operations in Washington helping them get tax breaks and government handouts. In short, their actions are controversial and newsworthy . . . or would be, if journalists covered them.

GE put MSNBC's headquarters in New Jersey after negotiating a deal whereby the state helped the company pay for new equipment and agreed to funnel back to GE 80 percent of the state income tax collected from MSNBC employees for a decade. My co-workers and I paid taxes that were "in effect refunded to profit-glutted" GE, in the words of Ralph Nader, who added, "Now that would have been a great *Donahue* show!" Somehow I couldn't get it on the air: "Top story tonight: Our boss is a welfare queen."

A few years ago Tom Brokaw made a speech in Minneapolis and was greeted by antiwar protesters critical of NBC's Iraq coverage; they accused NBC of a conflict-of-interest since GE profited from aircraft that were bombing Iraq. A local daily reported that Brokaw said "he did not know if GE-made weapons were used against Iraq." I've heard many elite journalists over the years virtually boast that they haven't a clue what their corporate parent does—a stunning admission of disinterest in powerful institutions that heavily influence politics and economics. Some journalists know about dubious conduct by their parent company and look away; most know not to look there in the first place.*

## CURTIS AND COHEN

One reason I didn't co-host my own MSNBC show is because management decided instead to bring *Curtis & Kuby* from talk radio to television—one of the oddest couples to come to TV since Felix and Oscar.

---

*In some other countries, journalists are imprisoned or killed for offending the powers that be. That's not the case in our country, where fear and timidity in corporate newsrooms seem so disproportionate to the risks . . . getting fired, career stagnation.

Rightwinger Curtis Sliwa is the street-smart, PR-savvy founder of the Guardian Angels, the volunteer safety brigades that patrol city streets and subways. Leftwinger Ron Kuby is a controversial criminal defense lawyer—whose "mommy is a commie," according to his standard introduction.

Curtis and Cohen

The duo had an arresting look for TV: the bearded, pony-tailed Kuby in his sport coat and tie, seated next to Sliwa in his red beret and glossy red Guardian Angels jacket. They had a fluid talk show shtick that might have seemed a bit comedic and wise-crackly for cable news. But MSNBC had long simulcast the Don Imus radio show in the mornings. Unlike the *Imus* show, *Curtis & Kuby* avoided racist and antigay fare.*

With me as Kuby's main substitute, the show became "Curtis and Cohen" roughly once a week through the summer and early fall of 2002. On our first show, Curtis explained that in the absence of his regular co-host, "another progressive Jewish lawyer" would be sitting in. I warned him on-air if he ever called *my* mommy a commie, she'd sue him—"if she doesn't have a heart attack first."

It was easy working with Curtis. On most topics, he'd provide a fervent, sometimes caricatured conservative stance, and my role was to follow up with any clarification of facts or issues, especially on legal matters. Curtis was a master of malapropism, a modern-day Slip Mahoney, and it was my job to fix those as well. On one show he referred to an "Alger Hiss story, rags to riches." "Not Alger Hiss," I piped in, "Horatio Alger." Seconds later he turned the mike over to an anchor with a difficult surname and apologized: "I bet I botulized your name."

---

*On *Imus*, gay people have been called "faggots," "lesbos" and "carpetmunchers." Imus once said that he hired an on-air sidekick "to do nigger jokes." When the *New York Times* assigned an African American woman to cover President Clinton, Imus remarked that the *Times* "lets the cleaning lady cover the White House." Such bigoted antics don't seem to bother regular Imus guests like Tom Brokaw, Tim Russert, columnist Tom Friedman, John McCain and Joe Lieberman.

On another show, he confused "that communist" Arlo Guthrie with his dad, Woody Guthrie, the leftist singer-songwriter of the 1930s and '40s. I corrected him. Curtis responded, "Woody, Arlo—they're all the same."

Since this was talk radio come to TV, we debated everything from big news like corporate scandals, D.C. politics and Iraq to edgier items such as a beauty school excluding transvestites and the radio shock jocks who broadcast a live sex act in a church.

On TV, two hours of talk is an eternity. I loved it. Discussions went on at length . . . and then we'd go at it again on many of the same topics in hour 2. Curtis was rightwing on foreign policy and most crime and social issues, but he had a populist streak on economic issues.

I hoped Jack Welch was watching GE's news channel as the two of us carried on about how giant corporations shafted average Americans by buying politicians in Washington. Curtis wanted to sic extra IRS agents on corporate America to "keep these big guys in line." When I railed against "boardroom bandits laughing all the way to the bank," while "workers are getting laid off, pensioners are getting screwed" and Washington fails "to protect the middle class," Curtis replied, "We're actually in solidarity on this point."

On one show, I noted that President Bush had recently gone to his corporate *base* and "raised $30 million in one day from big business lobbyists." Curtis didn't defend the practice, except to point out that corporate-oriented Democrats do the same—which was my cue to single out the 50-member Congressional Progressive Caucus for praise.

On social issues, he and I were usually miles apart, like when the Supreme Court approved drug tests for high schoolers in any extracurricular activity. Curtis applauded the ruling against a girl who was in her school's choir. "What are they worried about?" I asked. "If she tokes up, she'll sing off-key?" She was asked to pee with male teachers hovering nearby. In "the land of the free and the home of the brave," I decried what was happening to individuality and privacy: "We're telling people that their bodily fluids are no longer theirs. We're teaching kids to be obedient. In a democracy, you want people to be questioning authority."

Curtis was an avid supporter of invading Iraq. On a show in August 2002, when I pointed out that Bush Sr.'s national security chief Brent Scowcroft had just come out persuasively against an Iraq invasion as the wrong war at the wrong time, Curtis hailed that as proof that Bush Jr. was no puppet of Papa Bush and his military experts.

CURTIS: He obviously has a mind of his own.

COHEN: A very dangerous one.

After Curtis and I went at it, Jerry Falwell joined us as a guest. He claimed, without evidence, that Saddam "more than likely" had a hand in the 9/11 attacks. But Falwell gave a little ground when I asked him:

> We are going to war with enemies that used to be our allies: Osama bin Laden, Saddam Hussein. It seems to me if we didn't help build up dictators and terrorists when they're amassing power, then maybe we wouldn't have to sacrifice American soldiers and innocent people overseas. What do you say about the Reagan policy that so embraced Saddam Hussein during and after he used chemical weapons against his own people and against the Iranians?

Falwell replied, "You know, I'm not totally disagreeing with you there." Then he blamed the State Department (but not Reagan) for tending to "get in bed with the wrong guys."

★   ★   ★

Despite our divide on issues, Curtis and I shared the same annoyance with MSNBC's habit of going "live" when there was nothing newsworthy at the other end of the camera. The show was repeatedly interrupted for non-events, like the many law enforcement "pressers" in kidnapping cases where nothing new was announced—after which Curtis and I would speculate cluelessly about the event's meaning. I had prided myself on being a TV pundit scrupulous about only discussing topics I'd seriously thought about and researched. On live TV, one doesn't have that luxury. We're all telebimbos.

Curtis Sliwa is a master of infotainment, but our show sometimes ventured into the realm of "disinfotainment." The blame lay not so much with him but with MSNBC—like when our overblown kidnap coverage suggested an epidemic was gripping the nation.

Or when the anchor came on the air during our show with BREAKING NEWS attributed to Reuters: "An airliner has crashed at the airport in Nairobi. That's according to a control tower official. In addition, the television station KTN in Nairobi says 76 people are feared dead. That's all we know—apparently an airliner has gone down at the Nairobi Airport. . . . We'll keep you posted."

Five minutes later, the anchor came back with an update "on the plane crash in Nairobi, Kenya. . . . Television in Nairobi is saying 76 people feared dead, including an unnamed famous personality. Now whether that is someone of international stature or someone who is well-known within that country, it doesn't specify. . . . We're following that for you."

Thirty minutes later, the anchor returned with a final announcement:

> We have been reporting through Reuters news agency a plane crash at the Nairobi Airport in Nairobi, Kenya. [Map of Kenya displayed, titled "Plane Crash."] We are now learning from Kenyan police that there was no air crash. In fact, there was an alert that was caused by a security drill. . . . There was no crash in Nairobi, Kenya.

The story arrived with a bang and disappeared with a whimper. As Emily Litella would say on *Saturday Night Live*, "Never mind!"

★　★　★

July 2002 saw the birth of an activist effort in defense of domestic diva Martha Stewart, then facing a media frenzy and legal inquiry over insider trading. The "Save Martha" campaign took the media by storm, especially cable news. SaveMartha.com founder John Small, a clever marketing consultant, was interviewed on CNN, Fox News (repeatedly), MSNBC (repeatedly), CNBC, CBS News—going from studio to studio in a whirlwind tour.

Trying my best to look dignified

The intense coverage brought crowds of visitors to his website, where they could buy Save Martha buttons, shirts and aprons.

We interviewed Small on a "Curtis and Cohen" episode the day after he led a protest outside CBS studios (where Stewart's appearances on *The Early Show* had been suspended). If you caught our interview, you saw Curtis in his red beret . . . next to the activist in his Save Martha chef's hat, holding a cake . . . next to me, trying my best to look dignified. This was especially difficult after Curtis put a chef's hat over his beret, making him look like Beldar Conehead. We asked how many people had joined the recent Save Martha rally. "There were four of us there," said the protest leader, but he pledged to turn out "at least six people" at his next rally.

Three months after this bizarre interview, rallies seeking to stop an invasion of Iraq occurred across the country and the globe, with about 150,000 marching in Washington and San Francisco; four months after that came the biggest peace demonstrations in world history. Leaders of these huge protests got nothing close to the cable news platform afforded to Mr. Save Martha. Had they received such a friendly forum at MSNBC, producers would have been reprimanded.

I still remember what the Save Martha leader told us when we asked him about plans for any future demonstrations. Only one was planned, to celebrate Martha Stewart's upcoming birthday: "Cakes across America."

# CHAPTER SEVEN
## DRUMS OF WAR

September 11 made 2001 a defining year in our country's history. But 2002 may have been the strangest in history. It began with all eyes on Osama bin Laden and U.S. military efforts to capture or kill him in Afghanistan. It ended with Osama bin Forgotten—as the White House turned its attention to war against a different enemy, Iraq. In Bush's January 2003 State of the Union speech, Saddam Hussein was mentioned 17 times, Bin Laden not once.

Everything about my tenure at MSNBC occurred in the context of the ever-intensifying war drums over Iraq—the rise and fall of my on-air career, the rise and fall of *Donahue*, the rise and fall of debate on the channel. The war drums were beating sporadically and faintly when I arrived at MSNBC; they grew louder and louder as invasion day approached, until the din became so deafening that rational, journalistic thinking could not occur. To hear those drums today, all I have to do is picture myself at my desk at MSNBC.

For 19 weeks, I appeared in on-air debates almost every afternoon—the last weeks focusing on Iraq. Even at the end, I felt the need to clarify basic facts obscured in the media fog: "It wasn't Saddam Hussein who attacked us on Sept. 11; it was these religious fanatics in Al Qaeda who hate the secularist Saddam Hussein." I warned that invading Iraq would undermine "our coalition with Muslim and Arab countries that we need to fight Al Qaeda."

In October 2002, my debate segments were terminated. There was no room for me after MSNBC launched *Countdown: Iraq*—a daily one-hour show that seemed more keen on glamorizing a potential war than scrutinizing or debating it. *Countdown: Iraq* featured retired colonels and generals, sometimes resembling boys with war toys as they used props, maps and glitzy graphics to spin invasion scenarios.

They reminded me of pumped-up ex–football players doing pregame analysis and diagramming plays.

It was excruciating to be sidelined at MSNBC, watching so many nondebates in which myth and misinformation were served up unchallenged. Soon after my afternoon debates stopped, MSNBC cancelled *Curtis & Kuby*—so I lost even that platform. I had been effectively silenced. I'd evolved from media critic to media pundit . . . and back again to media critic. Except now I was seeing the bias and exclusion from a front-row seat inside a major news network.

On *Countdown: Iraq* and other prewar programming, military analysts typically appeared on the air alone and unopposed. Or they appeared in groups of two or three . . . unopposed. The thinking was that they were experts, not partisans. But the closeness of these retired military men to the Pentagon often obstructed independent, skeptical analysis.

In November 2002, when Hans Blix led United Nations weapons inspectors back into Iraq after a four-year absence, *Countdown: Iraq* host Lester Holt asked an MSNBC military analyst, "What's the buzz from the Pentagon about Hans Blix?" The retired colonel answered that Blix was considered "to be something like the Inspector Clousseau of the weapons of mass destruction inspection program. He's the kind of guy who will only remember the last thing he was told. That he's very malleable."*

Retired Gen. Barry McCaffrey (President Clinton's "drug czar") was the star military analyst on NBC and MSNBC, a hawk who loudly echoed White House claims of an Iraqi threat. His prewar analysis left viewers ill-prepared for what would follow a U.S. invasion. Weeks before the war started, he was upbeat about Pentagon planning: "I just got an update briefing from Secretary Rumsfeld and his team on what's the aftermath of the fighting. And I was astonished at the complexity and dedication with which they've gone about thinking through this: humanitarian aid, find the weapons of mass destruction, protect the population, jump-start an Iraqi free media. So a lot of energy has gone into this."

---

*The Pentagon's view of Blix may have been colored by Deputy Defense Secretary Paul Wolfowitz, who reportedly asked the CIA to dig for dirt on Blix months before he returned to Iraq. Blix got it right on Iraqi WMD. When it was later learned that U.S. intelligence had bugged Blix's UN office, he quipped, "I only wish they'd listened."

During the invasion, McCaffrey crowed, "Thank God for the Abrams tank and the Bradley fighting vehicle." Unknown to MSNBC viewers, the general sat on the boards of several military contracting corporations—including IDT, which pocketed millions for doing God's work on the Abrams and Bradley. (Still on NBC's payroll in mid-2005, Gen. McCaffrey remained stalwart on the nightly news about U.S. troops in Iraq and opposed a timetable for withdrawal.)

In a 1994 CNN debate about the overreliance on military analysts in war coverage, I had complained about a recurring pattern in which mainstream journalists, after each war, vow to be more skeptical when the next war comes: "Then when the next time comes—it's the same reporters interviewing the same experts, who buy the distortions from the Pentagon."

As the invasion of Iraq began in 2003, CNN news chief Eason Jordan admitted that his network's military analysts were government approved:

> I went to the Pentagon myself several times before the war started and met with important people there and said, for instance, at CNN, here are the generals we're thinking of retaining to advise us on the air and off about the war. And we got a big thumbs-up on all of them. That was important.

History was indeed repeating itself. CNN's admission of Pentagon-approved analysts brought to mind FAIR's protest chant: "Two, four, six, eight/Separate the press and state."

## TRUST US, WE'RE EXPERTS

The run-up to the Iraq war added a new wrinkle to TV news coverage. Along with the tried-and-true military analysts, each network featured "weapons experts"—usually without opposition or balance—to discuss the Bush team's main justification for war: Iraq's alleged possession of weapons of mass destruction.

The problem for journalism was that among WMD experts, there was a wide spectrum of views, including many who were skeptical of an Iraq weapons threat. The problem worsened when the UN sent new inspectors into Iraq who could not confirm any of the U.S. claims.

How did MSNBC and other networks solve the problem? They favored experts who backed the Bush view—and hired several of them as paid analysts. Networks that normally cherished shouting matches were opting for discussions of harmonious unanimity. This made for dull, predictable television. It also helped lead our nation to war based on false premises.

CNN and other outlets featured David Albright, a former UN inspector in Iraq who repeatedly asserted before the war that Iraq was in possession of chemical and biological weapons. Asked about his assertions after no WMD were found, Albright pointed his finger at the White House: "I certainly accepted the administration claims on chemical and biological weapons. I figured they were telling the truth."

Another CNN expert was former CIA analyst and Brookings fellow Kenneth Pollack, who fervently pushed for war, telling TV audiences that Iraq "has biological and chemical weapons." He warned *Oprah* viewers that Saddam could use WMD against the U.S. homeland and was "building new capabilities as fast as he can." Later, he blamed his errant remarks about Iraq's WMD on a "consensus" in the intelligence community: "That was not me making that claim; that was me parroting the claims of so-called experts."

To be fair, TV news was not alone in trumpeting the WMD threat. The *New York Times* and reporter Judith Miller led the journalistic pack with a string of page 1 scare stories based on disreputable sources. Miller's main source, unnamed, was Iraqi exile Ahmed Chalabi, who waged a disinformation campaign to convince the U.S. to invade Iraq. "He has provided most of the front-page exclusives on WMD to our paper," Miller wrote in an internal email that leaked. After war began and no weapons were found, Chalabi gloated to a London daily, "We are heroes in error. As far as we're concerned, we were entirely successful."

★ ★ ★

MSNBC relied heavily on two weapons experts as paid analysts. One was Richard Butler, an Australian who had led UN inspectors in Iraq in 1997 and '98. Although not hawkish about a U.S. invasion of Iraq, he appeared on show after show before the war to assert that Iraq currently possessed WMD and was hiding them from UN inspectors.

The weapons expert who appeared most frequently on MSNBC and NBC was David Kay. Almost never was Kay balanced by an opposing view. In dozens of appearances in the months before the war, Kay spoke with certainty that Iraq possessed WMD. Like the Bush administration, he consistently pushed for war and belittled the chances that UN inspections could work in Iraq—"a country the size of California" (Dec. '02), "the size of France" (Nov. '02), "twice the size of the state of Idaho" (Sept. '02). Waiting for a new round of UN inspections was a "trap," according to Kay.

Sometimes bias is left vs. right. This time it was right vs. wrong—and MSNBC's main expert was relentlessly, breathtakingly wrong. Kay was wrong when he pointed to Iraqi drones as WMD dispensers; they were actually for reconnaissance. He was wrong on aluminum tubes that the White House claimed could only be used in developing nuclear weapons. He was wrong on Iraq's "nuclear program." Introducing Kay on MSNBC's *Hardball*, Chris Matthews gushed, "He's a former weapons inspector. He knows what he's talking about in Iraq."*

A week before the war started, Kay made his umpteenth appearance on *Countdown: Iraq* and warned against last-minute diplomatic efforts that might give Iraqis a delay and avert a U.S. invasion: "The only test that makes very much sense . . . is for Saddam Hussein to go on television and say, 'All these years I've been lying; I really do have weapons of mass destruction.' It's very hard to see how they can do that." Indeed.

On day 2 of the war, an upbeat Kay appeared alongside NBC's Tom Brokaw to reiterate his view that inspections "could not disarm Iraq"; he predicted that U.S. soldiers would in due time find chemical weapons, "stockpiles of VX and mustard gas," and biological "warheads and aerial bombs."

---

*In a January 2003 segment of *Countdown: Iraq*, Gen. McCaffrey appeared alongside Kay (how's that for opposing views?). McCaffrey responded to Lester Holt's question about 12 empty shells found that day by inspectors in Baghdad: "I start with an assumption, Lester—David Kay is the expert on this—that there are thousands of gallons of mustard agents, serin, nerve agent VX still in Iraq. They're hidden. There are thousands of shells."

After eight weeks, nothing had been found except a couple of trailers that U.S. officials were eyeing as mobile biological weapons labs. This led to a dramatic NBC scoop starring network analyst Kay, who

was rushed to one of the trailers in Iraq to do an on-air assessment: "This is where the biological process took place. You took the nutrients—think of it sort of as the chicken soup for biological weapons." Kay insisted there was no other use for the trailer except cooking up bioweapons: "Literally, there's nothing else you would do this way on a mobile facility."

NBC's David Kay assesses trailer in Iraq.

He was wrong again. The trailers were not weapons labs. They were basically harmless—used to produce hydrogen for military weather balloons.

With U.S. troops empty-handed in the hunt for WMD, David Kay gave up his NBC/MSNBC post to take a full-time government job— not exactly a great leap, given the role he'd played as a White House echo. Kay was hired to lead the Iraq Survey Group, organized by the CIA and Pentagon to scour Iraq for WMD. U.S. soldiers died protecting his posse, but the search turned up nothing.

"We were all wrong," Kay reported to the U.S. Senate in January 2004.

## SMEARS, CENSORS AND CELEBRITIES

Not every weapons expert had been wrong. Take Scott Ritter, an ex-Marine and Gulf War veteran who gained fame in 1997 as a hard-nosed UN inspector in Iraq. In the last months of 2002, he told any audience or journalist who would hear him that Iraqi WMD represented no threat to our country and that biological or chemical weapons once possessed by Iraq would have degraded over time. "Send in the inspectors," urged Ritter, "don't send in the Marines."

It's telling that in the run-up to the war, no American TV network hired any on-air analysts from among the experts who questioned White House WMD claims. None would hire Ritter.*

Inside MSNBC in 2002, Ritter was the target of a smear that he was receiving covert funds from Saddam Hussein's government. The slur, obviously aimed at reducing his appearances, insinuated that Ritter's views were not genuine and heartfelt, but procured. The "covert funding" charge surfaced repeatedly at MSNBC, especially when we sought to book Ritter as a guest on *Donahue*.

The charge actually aired on a September 2002 show hosted by MSNBC editor-in-chief Jerry Nachman, who claimed—without offering any evidence—that the Iraqi government had funded Ritter's current trip to Iraq: "He's there on their dime."

The irony is that MSNBC at the time regularly featured another commentator who would soon be receiving covert government funds. The covert funder was the Bush administration, specifically its Education Department—which, beginning in 2003, paid pundit Armstrong Williams nearly a quarter-million dollars to promote Bush's No Child Left Behind Act. The Bush team broke its promise to fully fund the Act but kept faith with the pundit. When I repeatedly debated Williams at MSNBC, I had no idea that he'd be part of a *No Pundit Left Behind* program.

★ ★ ★

Days after Nachman falsely accused Ritter of traveling to Iraq on Saddam's dime, we at the *Donahue* show booked foreign policy critic Ramsey Clark as an in-studio guest. The former U.S. attorney general denounced Bush's Iraq policy. Soon after, I was told it wasn't supposed to happen; MSNBC bosses had Clark on some sort of blacklist.

---

*Songwriter Jackson Browne has noted that it's "easier sometimes to change the past." Cable news is good at rewriting history: In July 2005, conservative MSNBC host Tucker Carlson pretended there hadn't been any WMD skeptics before the war: "Just for the record, I would point out that everyone was wrong about WMDs. Not just Judy Miller, but me and you and you and everybody in the Western world, including Hillary Clinton."

★　★　★

TV's big broadcast networks were no more open to critical voices, as illustrated by FAIR's study of the nightly newscasts on CBS, NBC, ABC and PBS in the week before and the week after Colin Powell's bellicose UN Security Council presentation on Iraqi WMD. Powell's February 2003 speech was built on obvious exaggerations and false-hoods. But nightly news viewers would have been largely clueless. Of the 393 people interviewed about Iraq during those crucial weeks, only three were antiwar advocates. That's a fraction of 1 percent—a nondebate, at a time when polls showed half the country opposing a rush to war.

★　★　★

Informed, articulate, full-time antiwar leaders and U.S. foreign policy critics are not hard to find. The Institute for Public Accuracy provides their names and phone numbers to thousands of journalists week after week. But, unlike "military analysts" and "weapons experts," peace advocates are not warmly regarded or welcomed at cable news.

On *Donahue*, we booked a number of them as guests . . . but almost always balanced by a louder hawk or two. Some were booked on Fox News, where O'Reilly and Hannity could be expected to question their patriotism or shout them down. Most antiwar advocates will get fewer solo appearances on cable news in their lifetimes than the Save Martha leader got in a couple of weeks.

There is one giant exception to this rule: Hollywood celebrities. In December 2002, a group of 100 actors, musicians and writers called "Artists United to Win Without War"—including Ed Asner, Jackson Browne, Don Cheadle, Matt Damon, Danny Glover, Helen Hunt, Jessica Lange, Téa Leoni, Dave Matthews, Susan Sarandon and Martin Sheen—sent a sober letter to President Bush urging "rigorous UN weapons inspections to assure Iraq's effective disarmament" and opposing "a pre-emptive military invasion of Iraq" that "will make us less, not more, secure."

Finally the gatekeepers of cable news opened their doors wide to antiwar voices . . . as long as they came attached to famous faces. Janeane Garofalo and Mike Farrell were two actors bold enough to say yes even to the O'Reillys and Hannitys.

Since by then I was pretty much off the air, I found myself on the sidelines—or upstairs in MSNBC's workout room—rooting for these surrogates. On cable news, the actors became spokespersons for millions of largely voiceless Americans who opposed the drive toward war.

On MSNBC's *Nachman* show, Garofalo was interrogated about whether she felt advocacy-minded celebrities were sufficiently informed on their chosen issues. It was a thrill to see Garofalo turn the tables on Nachman and his booking choices: "I wish I wasn't the one talking to you. I wish there was somebody who's better informed than me, like Scott Ritter, former UN weapons inspector, who is on-board with Winning Without War. I wish that [former assistant secretary of defense] Lawrence Korb was here. I wish that [former U.S. ambassador] Ed Peck was here. Because I'm sure that they could be much more articulate and make much more substantive points than I can."

Garofalo was evidently unaware that Nachman had smeared Ritter on the air as Saddam's paid puppet.

## WHAT IF IT'S NOT TRUE?

One of the great cable news standoffs of the prewar period involved actor Mike Farrell and Dan Abrams, who hosts MSNBC's sometimes-lurid legal affairs show and suffers from bouts of O'Reillyitis. No anchor on cable news is quicker to a celebrity trial than Abrams. The good news is he had a face made for television—young, strong-jawed. (Nachman, it was said around MSNBC, had "a face made for radio.") The bad news is that on the day Abrams interviewed Farrell—Dec. 12, 2002—the youthful host had become enchanted by the latest tall tale from Bush officials.

I watched the show on an MSNBC stationary bike, with my heart rate soaring less from my pedaling than because someone on national TV was finally expressing skepticism about an Iraq scare story planted in the mainstream media.

Note to journalism students: Get the *Abrams Report* transcript and scrutinize it as a case study in what *not* to do.

Referring to Farrell as "a Hollywood star who is leading the anti-war effort," Abrams opened the show by saying:

> Does the U.S. now have the proof it needs to attack Iraq? The
> *Washington Post* reports that, within the past few weeks, Iraq may
> have sold or given a chemical weapon, possibly nerve gas, to
> Islamic extremists affiliated with Al Qaeda. The *Post* quotes what

they refer to as knowledgeable officials speaking without permission who describe it as a credible report, but not backed up
by definitive evidence.

I checked my dictionary to translate "*knowledgeable officials speaking
without permission who describe it as a credible report, but not backed up by
definitive evidence*" from journalese into plain English. It said: "1. hoax-
ers 2. disinformers (See Karl Rove)." Aside from facts and credibility,
the *Post* story had all the elements of a White House wet dream: Al
Qaeda–Iraq link, WMD in Iraq, recent dissemination of WMD.

Abrams began his Farrell interview by saying, "This new report in-
dicates to me that this, if true, is a very, very serious issue that might
warrant a war with Iraq."

> FARRELL: Sure. Let me, if I might, ask you to back up just a bit.
> "If true," you said.
>
> ABRAMS: Right.
>
> FARRELL: What if it's *not* true?

For all the ridicule aimed at antiwar actors that week on talk radio
and cable news, here was an actor posing the right question to a jour-

nalist whose credulity was vast
and memory short. The *Post* story
had come out after other leaked
stories about Iraq had been debunked—from a phantom Iraqi–
Al Qaeda meeting in Prague to
the hoax that Iraq was importing
aluminum tubes to restart its
phantom nuclear program.

Farrell suggested that Bush
officials might have put out the
leak "so that you and others can
raise it on television and ratchet

Farrell challenges Iraq war.

up again people's fears. If this report is *not* true, what does it mean?
And what does it mean to those of us in America who feel that perhaps this administration, as has been called the most secretive in U.S.
history, is simply trying to gull us into approving an action that goes
against the very principles upon which our democracy is based?"

Abrams was undeterred. He came back at Farrell with three more versions of the "if it's true" question. The actor (whose job is fictional portrayals) stood firm in encouraging the journalist (whose job is to deal in facts) to be skeptical. Farrell then criticized U.S. media for "acting as a megaphone for the administration throughout this process."

After a commercial break, Abrams remained as fixated on the *Post* story as a cat on a shiny, swinging object:

> I'm joined again by actor Mike Farrell. And before the break, we were talking about this new report that seems to indicate that Saddam Hussein or Iraq may have—may have—given chemical weapons to Al Qaeda. It is considered a credible report, but it is an uncorroborated report. And we were talking about whether this would change his position.

Now Farrell teed off on the words *"credible but uncorroborated"*— and again warned that the story was likely another trumped-up "scare tactic" from the administration.

Farrell was offered the last word in the segment.

> ABRAMS: I'll give you the last five seconds. Go ahead.

> FARRELL: Is it important to you that the administration has lied in the past and that we have indications that they're continuing to try and gull us into believing that they are telling the truth?

> ABRAMS: I don't know about that.

The next morning, the *New York Times* reported that "senior administration officials" had "discounted" the *Post* story about Iraq handing weapons to terrorists. In two days, the story vanished even from the *Post*, never to raise its ugly head again. It was yet another hoax. But the story, which dominated cable news hour after hour, had apparently served its purpose—having been leaked, as Farrell correctly warned Abrams, "so that you and others can raise it on television and ratchet up again people's fears."

I never saw Abrams offer his viewers an apology or explanation. More important, there is no evidence that he or anyone at MSNBC investigated how such a hollow story had hijacked a news channel. Farrell's $64,000 question was never answered: "If this report is *not* true, what does it mean?"

★  ★  ★

In 2004, the *New York Times* and *Washington Post* each offered quasi-apologies ("mini culpas," to borrow a phrase from *Slate*) about their gullible coverage of prewar WMD claims. Cable news offered no such apologies. This despite the fact that no other news medium—except rightwing talk radio—had been as persistently wrong.*

Appearing at a 2004 Harvard forum, CBS's then-anchor Dan Rather was asked about inadequacies in TV news coverage in the run-up to the Iraq war. After acknowledging that more questions could have been put to the White House, Rather made a comment that reflects the attitude of too many media heavyweights:

> Look, when a president of the United States, any president,
> Republican or Democrat, says these are the facts, there is heavy
> prejudice, including my own, to give him the benefit of any doubt.
> And for that I do not apologize.

★  ★  ★

Ninety years ago, Austrian scholar Karl Kraus wrote, "How is the world ruled and led to war? Diplomats lie to journalists and believe these lies when they see them in print." Or, updating Kraus, when they see them on TV.

## MILITARY-TV-INDUSTRIAL COMPLEX

War is good for business. It's good for firms that service U.S. troops in faraway lands like Halliburton, Dick Cheney's old company. It's good for GE, which made a financial killing in the first Gulf War from weapons and reconstruction contracts—and was profiting from the latest round of war. It's good for the military contracting firms on whose boards sits retired Gen. Barry McCaffrey, the NBC analyst. A powerful corporate sector has long profited from war and war prep. President Eisenhower (a former general) warned about the influence

---

*TV news lacks even a correction box. Imagine a cable news channel, utilizing its website and 24/7 status, that boldly offered corrections and actively solicited real-time criticism and genuine debate about its coverage. Such a Web feature could be a huge success . . . yet is unthinkable in today's cable news environment.

of this "military-industrial complex" just before exiting the White House at the height of the Cold War in 1961.

With the end of the Cold War and the loss of our decades-long Soviet enemy, there was momentarily high anxiety among military-contracting companies. Then Iraq invaded Kuwait in August 1990. At a gathering of Pentagon contractors in Milwaukee weeks later, the welcoming speaker won applause and cheers with his opening words: "Thank you, Saddam Hussein!"

War is also good for TV ratings. No one in cable news has ever forgotten the boost CNN got from the 1991 Gulf War in audience and stature. As 2003 neared, MSNBC was banking on a new war in Iraq. "America's News Channel" had run out of options: fervent coverage of kidnappings and Beltway snipers would cause a short-term uptick in ratings, but MSNBC was mired in last place among the three cable news channels. The press was reporting that GE was losing patience and might "pull the plug" on the channel—that GE doesn't stay in an industry unless its business is number one or two in that industry.

Inside MSNBC's newsroom, it was clear that war had become the centerpiece of management's ratings strategy. We could see it in who was hired and who removed; in the birth of *Countdown: Iraq* as *Donahue* was squelched; in the diminishing of dissent even as the public remained divided. What originated as a subtly felt *need for war* seemed to evolve into an on-air *push for war*. And the push grew stronger as Washington's war drums beat louder.

You didn't need to be inside MSNBC to catch the drift. In January 2003, *Baltimore Sun* television writer David Folkenflik reported that "GE's CEO, Jeffrey R. Immelt, said he'd like MSNBC to pursue the brasher Fox model. . . . Now, as attention to the fight against Al Qaeda has subsided in favor of reporting on the potential conflict against Hussein's forces, MSNBC airs a daily news program titled *Countdown: Iraq*. (CNN offers the almost identically titled *Showdown: Iraq*.) The result is coverage that presumes war is imminent and frequently ignores nuance and omits debate."

Folkenflik noted that cable news had "largely ignored" October's mass demonstrations against an Iraq invasion: "The strength of the protest didn't fit neatly into a narrative of a country girding for war, and it took many news outlets by surprise. CNN anchor Wolf Blitzer wondered aloud whether the press had dismissed the protest too quickly. 'If we do too much coverage of a potential war with Iraq, we're almost looking like we're anxious for the war to develop,' he said."

★  ★  ★

Back in July 2002, British prime minister Tony Blair convened a high-level meeting of top aides about Iraq. Minutes of the meeting reveal that Britain's intelligence chief had found a "perceptible shift in attitude" during his recent trip to Washington: "Military action was now seen as inevitable . . . justified by the conjunction of terrorism and WMD. But the intelligence and facts were being fixed around the policy."

When the top-secret minutes—dubbed "the Downing Street Memo"—leaked to the British press in May 2005, many people in the UK and the United States were outraged over evidence that the White House was committed to war eight months before the invasion, and that intelligence was being "fixed" to justify its stance. But top U.S. news media were blasé about the memo, and several justified their minimal coverage by saying the memo was *old news*; after all, it was "conventional wisdom" by summer 2002 that the Bush administration was committed to war. (Never mind that the White House publicly proclaimed month after month that war was "a last resort" and no decision had been made.)*

The truth is that the media elite typically know much that the public doesn't. With sources at the pinnacles of government power, media executives knew way before the rest of us that war was indeed coming, and when. Like military contractors who need notification about adding production shifts with the advent of war, the TV networks of GE and Murdoch and Time Warner had to make major investments toward the coming war.

In this regard, I'll never forget a 2001 *New York* magazine profile on NBC's Washington bureau chief Tim Russert that described him as a "confidant" of Jack Welch, then GE's CEO:

> When Welch wants to know what's going on in Washington (GE runs a mighty lobbying effort), he calls Russert, who tells him who's saying what to whom. Russert is, in other words, not just a senior guy in the NBC news division, but a significant GE asset in Washington.

---

*The Downing Street Memo went on to say, "It seemed clear that Bush had made up his mind to take military action. . . . But the case was thin. Saddam was not threatening his neighbours, his WMD capability was less than that of Libya, North Korea or Iran." And: "There was little discussion in Washington of the aftermath after military action."

★ ★ ★

I was a *Fox News Watch* regular when the district attorney of Boulder, Colorado, announced that he would *not* make an indictment in the JonBenet Ramsey murder. The decision shook cable news, which had shamelessly exploited the story (and its soft-core kiddie-porn footage) for ratings. An indictment and trial would have been a ratings bonanza. I joked on *News Watch* that the DA's decision might cause "mass suicides" among cable news executives.

Had war with Iraq been averted somehow at the last minute, I didn't expect suicides among MSNBC executives. Just firings. Or that GE might finally pull the plug on the channel.

## SADDAM ON THE GRASSY KNOLL

Seven weeks before the war began, I made my final MSNBC appearance—on a show that seemed to be the hosting debut of former GOP representative Joe Scarborough. In MSNBC's revolving door, hawks were flocking in as doves were cast out.

The star of the panel discussion was not Scarborough, but überhawk Frank Gaffney, a Reagan Defense Department official appearing as a guest from Washington. An MSNBC decision-maker had decided to feature Gaffney's charge that Iraq was not only involved with Al Qaeda and 9/11 but that Iraq was (I'm not joking) behind Timothy McVeigh and the Oklahoma City bombing. It was a fitting topic on which to end my on-air career at MSNBC. As the war drew closer, the rationales for war were growing nuttier.

After reading every available Internet article by conspiracists who placed Saddam in Oklahoma City, I opined to producers preshow that the claim was absurd and that valuable airtime shouldn't be wasted. But the goal, it seemed, was generating heat, not light.

I was not a happy camper when Scarborough opened the show with an unchallenged soundbite from Bush's State of the Union speech made the previous night that "Saddam Hussein aids and protects terrorists, including members of Al Qaeda. Secretly, and without fingerprints, he could provide one of his hidden weapons to terrorists." (We'd heard that one before.)

And I didn't get any happier when Gaffney referred to "important evidence" of Iraqi involvement in both the 1993 World Trade Center

Urging Gaffney to seek professional help

bombing and Oklahoma City—which he failed to enumerate beyond total gibberish.*

As the show proceeded, it became clear that Gaffney was serving up yet another reason for war—historical research, to determine if Saddam and Tim McVeigh were indeed co-conspirators: "The point here, gentlemen, is—we are not going to know the facts here unless and until we're inside the secret bunkers and files of Iraq. And I hope that will happen soon."

"Let's not start another war based on lies," I responded. "We've been to so many wars that way, where it was based on pretext." I derided Gaffney for trying to blame Saddam for "two of the most investigated crimes of the 20th century"—Oklahoma City and the '93 World Trade bombing.

The discussion was lurid even for cable news. I called Gaffney's claims "garbage" and suggested he was "in need of psychiatric care." I wasn't proud of myself as I left the studio. In fact, I was ashamed . . . for agreeing to take part in the Gaffney segment in the first place. I had done so to be a team player; I was, after all, a paid MSNBC contributor expected to punditize on the topic assigned me.

After the blowout, I lingered in the makeup room, embarrassed, when the show's young producer burst in. I started to apologize. But he was upbeat. He liked the debate: "Lots of energy!"

Scarborough had ended the discussion by saying, "We need you back here like for an hour or two with boxing gloves on. We are looking forward to having you back."

---

*Gaffney's "evidence," as stated on MSNBC: "Elements of [Iraqi] history need to be addressed, like the involvement of this Ramzi Yousef, clearly, I believe, tied to Iraq in both the World Trade Center and the Oklahoma City bombing. You have got Iraqi nationals in Oklahoma even to this day, but some of whom were involved, I believe clearly, with Timothy McVeigh and Terry Nichols. You have got evidence that one of them went on from there to Logan Airport, where he may have been casing the place for the subsequent attacks for Sept. 11."

I never appeared again on MSNBC. Gaffney remains a regular there and at the other cable news channels. If you're wild and wacky and on the right wing—whether a Gaffney or Ann Coulter or Jerry Falwell—you'll find a home in cable news, and no outlandish statements will be held against you.

★ ★ ★

Most Americans, especially conservatives, like to say that they favor *meritocracy*—"a system in which advancement is based on individual ability or achievement." But cable news is almost the opposite: a *kakistocracy*—a system in which "the least qualified or most unprincipled" rise to the top. Literally, it means "rule by the worst." In cable news, advancement clearly has little to do with one's achievements in providing accurate journalism.

If you study prewar TV news coverage, you'll notice something striking about the few pundits, hosts and experts who were correct on the war—who questioned WMD "evidence" and Iraq–Al Qaeda "links"; who warned of the chaos that would follow an invasion and challenged predictions that Iraqis would welcome U.S. troops as liberators. For the most part, these intrepid souls—persisting in the face of smears and charges of disloyalty—were spat out of TV and banished.

By contrast, those who dutifully echoed White House hyperbole and hoaxes in the prewar period have seen their TV careers flourish. I'm not aware of a single host, pundit or news executive who lost their job for getting such a huge story so totally wrong—as almost all of them did.

In cable news, one host fought the hardest—in the face of management obstruction—to ask the right questions and present the most informed, independent experts. His name was Phil Donahue. His show lasted seven months. He was terminated 22 days before the Iraq war began.

That story has yet to be told.

# CHAPTER EIGHT
## *DONAHUE* LAUNCHES

July 15, 2002—"I got a show," roared the host on opening night. "Holy cow, somehow a liberal got in!"

For MSNBC, hiring Phil Donahue was a desperation Hail Mary pass at the end of a football game. Lineup changes had been constant for years, but nothing had succeeded and time seemed to be running out.

Everyone signed off on the Donahue hire—MSNBC and NBC News brass, NBC chief Bob Wright, even GE CEO Jeff Immelt. Consensus did not imply confidence. Executives were nervous over the hire and anxious about Phil's politics. Sure, he was a huge star, one of the most famous faces in the history of talk TV. But in cable news, hiring an outspoken advocate from the left to host a nightly show was unheard of—rarer than a portsider hosting talk radio.

Left and pseudo-left voices were heard on cable news . . . as sidekicks to forceful co-hosts roaring on the right wing. Phil would be flying solo. Previously, the partisan solo hosts on MSNBC had been conservatives like Laura Ingraham and Alan Keyes. NBC boss Wright was himself a political conservative who saw CNN as liberal; it was Wright who in 1993 first made Roger Ailes a network president—at GE-owned CNBC, while Ailes was also the boss of Rush Limbaugh's syndicated TV show.

MSNBC hired Phil in April 2002, but the show didn't launch for three months. The lag only heightened the nervousness among NBC/MSNBC executives. In the interim, the political/media landscape shifted dramatically, with the real likelihood that our country would soon be at war with Iraq. *Donahue* went on the air just days before Prime Minister Tony Blair and his top aides held their secret meeting to discuss a U.S. attack on Iraq "now seen as inevitable"—in the words of the Downing Street Memo.

The Bush administration was marching half-cocked to war, and GE's cable news channel was about to showcase a blaring antiwar advocate as its top host. Holy F-16!

## FEAR IN SUITVILLE

As the *Donahue* debut approached, NBC/MSNBC brass—"Suitville," Phil called them—managed their anxiety about Phil's politics in various ways. One was denial: they pretended he was just a popular broadcaster without strong and controversial views. This denial led to a ridiculously lavish and *untargeted* prelaunch promo campaign, costing $1 million according to *Broadcasting & Cable*.

Not one dollar was aimed at Phil's natural audience for a cable news show—progressives, *Mother Jones* and *Nation* readers, etc. My proposals to earmark a few dollars for inexpensive, targeted advertising to these groups were rejected.

When Ailes launched Fox News, ad buys were targeted, with spots running regularly on Limbaugh's radio show. Ailes understood that cable news is *narrowcasting* and that a niche audience of a million right-leaning viewers would make Fox News a huge success. Compared to Ailes, our Suitville was inhabited by amateurs who'd convinced themselves that since Phil had been a broadcast star, he could somehow bring a vast, nonpolitical audience to a cable news outlet that rarely attracted 350,000 viewers. MSNBC's Suits were in broadcast mode—getting creamed by Ailes who knew he was narrowcasting.

Along with denial, MSNBC executives acted on their and their bosses nervousness about Phil's political views through suppression. Before our launch and for months after, management gave us one order beyond all others: "Be balanced." It was their mantra. We rarely heard directives to "be different" or "be exciting." But we had to ensure that Phil's viewpoint did not dominate; *Donahue* could not be seen as "a liberal show."

The promises made to me by MSNBC brass before I took the job about a progressive-angled show had been shattered—there was now no intention of offering clear counterprogramming against Fox.

Reasons for the "balance" obsession were not explained. The king of cable news, Bill O'Reilly, dominated our timeslot with a one-sided, opinionated show that thrived on its absence of balance. And he was on the most watched news channel, Fox, whose high ratings had been attributed to various factors—but never balance. Our country was evenly divided: half red, half blue. If Fox could build a small but profitable audience largely among reds, certainly we could build an audience—for one measly hour a night—largely among blues.

Since the balance order made no sense in terms of audience-building, I was not alone in suspecting that it was less about viewers than about the personal queasiness of GE/NBC executives over having hired an unabashed left host. On a cable news channel that would have let Phil offer vibrant, unfettered opposition to Bushworld each night, we could have grown a sizeable audience, especially as war approached. No such channel existed.

★  ★  ★

I was at MSNBC as a *Donahue* senior producer because Phil trusted me and wanted me nearby. It was that trust that management hoped to exploit in their efforts to bully him. "Phil will listen to you" was their refrain. "If it comes from you, he'll hear it." I brushed off the steady pleas to sell Phil on the need for balance and evenhandedness and asking tough "devil's advocate" questions of like-minded guests. Our chief rival, O'Reilly, was known for strong interrogations . . . of adversaries, not guests he agreed with. But MSNBC Suits were scared witless that Phil might appear too soft on progressives and peaceniks.

## PUMP UP THE VOLUME

Our first guest on our first show was former UN weapons inspector Scott Ritter, whose prewar skepticism about Iraqi WMD proved totally correct. That's the good news. The bad news is that—to appease management—he was "balanced" by not one but two war hawks: Senator James Imhofe and Iraqi exile Ahmed Chalabi, a key source for U.S. journalists and prime fabricator of the Iraq WMD threat. The resulting debate generated lots of "energy" and crosstalk as Ritter faced a double-barreled barrage of dubious claims (and some devil's advocacy).

> DONAHUE: [Saddam's] gathering weapons of mass destruction—bombs and weapons. He's already gassed the Kurds. We've got to do it. He's going to send a nuclear—
>
> RITTER: Phil, where are the weapons?

Ritter to Chalabi: "You're making this up."

Chalabi joined the debate from London. He and Ritter continually spoke over each other as Chalabi insisted on telling viewers of Ritter's beliefs: "You know Saddam has chemical weapons," said the Iraqi exile. "I don't know that," replied Ritter.

CHALABI: You knew that Saddam had VX, had weaponized it and had put it on missile warheads.

RITTER: That were destroyed.

(CROSSTALK)

RITTER: They were destroyed warheads. They were destroyed factories.

CHALABI: There were tons of precursors.

RITTER: That were destroyed.

Ritter and Chalabi bickered about a training camp in Iraq.

CHALABI: It is a terrorist training center with biological weapons facilities and chemical weapons facilities.

RITTER: Absolutely not. You're making this up.

CHALABI: Of course it is.

RITTER: You're making this up.

Ritter aimed questions at the senator: "You want to go to war; you want to commit our troops. Where are the facts that he has weapons? I'm tired of you and others saying that you know that he has chemical weapons, biological weapons, nuclear weapons. Put the facts on the table. . . . Where are the weapons?" He challenged the senator: "Make a case for war before you send our troops off."

Imhofe didn't provide facts, but he did pull rank, citing his own expertise and that of his colleagues on high.

SEN. IMHOFE: Those of us who are on the intelligence committee and the President and Don Rumsfeld and his 13 people on the Rumsfeld Commission, who are the most knowledgeable nuclear experts, all say that he has this capability.

RITTER: Prove it.

Although outnumbered, Ritter was unmoved: "I would say that before we go to war, we better be darn sure that he's got these weapons and he represents a threat. It has to be more than politically motivated."

★ ★ ★

Our second show focused on a crucial and rarely covered topic at the time: the PATRIOT Act and post-9/11 assaults on Constitutional liberties. The show was marred by a rabid rightwing guest who repeatedly interrupted other guests; he was there to satisfy management demands for "balance." Viewers complained about the interruptions and crosstalk—the beginning of what would become a torrent of criticism from progressives expressing concerns about *Donahue*.

★ ★ ★

Although our early shows included powerful segments, I sensed that *Donahue* was off course from the beginning, with Phil miscast as a referee of rancorous debates. So did TV critics, who complained about "senseless screaming matches" and "headache-making TV." *Boston Globe* media writer Mark Jurkowitz predicted the show would fail with Phil as just "another ringmaster for politically polarizing shouting heads"—but could succeed if he's allowed to provide a coherent "forum for unpopular views on hot-button subjects."

My ideas for adjusting course would have tilted the show leftward. I proposed that night in and night out we feature Phil-type advocates rarely seen on television and Phil-type topics ("You pay taxes—why doesn't Enron?"; "Is Iraq the next Vietnam?"), unapologetically framed as oppositional and populist TV. To me, this was the only path to success: building our base among viewers seeking "the anti-Fox," and recruiting them through targeted ads, independent media and the Internet.

Management rejected such an approach as "too strident." I could almost hear Roger Ailes laughing from across the Hudson.

My "senior producer" title at *Donahue* was somewhat overblown. Initially, I had a hand in guest selection and briefing Phil on potential questions or points he might raise on-air. It was a joy to see some eloquent, independent experts on national TV—and to see Phil asking powerful guests questions no one else would ask. But my role diminished over time, as the Suits steadily seized control of the show.

## BE LARRY, BE CONNIE, ANYONE BUT PHIL

Our huge opening night ratings—inflated by the ad blitz—quickly receded, as viewers uninterested in serious issues saw this wasn't going to be fun daytime entertainment. The drop-off was completely predictable. But the Suits went into a panic, having convinced themselves that their overnight ticket out of the cellar was a huge ad campaign, a famous face and a miraculous conversion of middle-America into cable news junkies.

We needed to go niche, to differentiate *Donahue* from the rest of cable news—indeed, the rest of television. But that was impossible because of a dizzying succession of orders from a frantic management. First, the balance command was reducing some of our best segments to incomprehensible food fights. Next, we were told to do more "news of the day" segments (child kidnappings, weird crime cases), which didn't captivate Phil and played straight into the only strength of our competitor on CNN, Connie Chung. We could never "out-Connie" Connie on crime or tabloid stories. Later, we were told to interview nonpolitical celebrities (Dr. Phil, *America's Most Wanted* host John Walsh), as if we could "out-Larry" Larry King.

Instead of letting Phil be Phil, MSNBC was prodding a TV original to imitate others. On his daytime show, Phil got huge ratings while showcasing issues he was passionate about . . . and partisan about. Balance was no more required on daytime *Donahue* than on *The O'Reilly Factor*. He took advocates he believed in—like Ralph Nader, Gloria Steinem and Jesse Jackson—and helped make them household faces in the Heartland.

If Phil had his way, he would have been making household faces of today's most articulate progressives—folks like Amy Goodman, Medea Benjamin, Cornel West, Naomi Klein. I submitted lists of dozens of such advocates; a few made it on the air, sometimes only to be outshouted by the obligatory RR (rabid rightist). These progressives are as engaging as the rightwing guests who populate cable news (Coulter, Gaffney, Falwell)—with the added advantage of being factual. This is the show I joined Phil to work on and naively hoped MSNBC might allow. But what you could do a few years ago in syndicated TV is not permitted nowadays on cable news.

After we'd been on the air several weeks, I asked a *Donahue* boss—who was in a position to know—what was behind management's balance obsession and constraints on Phil: "The rap on us is that we're anti-American."

It was as if we'd hurtled back 50 years to the beginnings of TV . . . amid the McCarthy witch hunts.

## BRIGHT MOMENTS

Despite the obstacles put in front of us by management, *Donahue* was able to create some unique and compelling television—a credit to Phil and hardworking producers striving to go beyond typical cable news fare. Much of our best programming occurred in the first weeks of the show.

In week 2, in front of a Houston audience filled with laid-off Enron employees, Phil led an emotional and informative town meeting on corporate crime—featuring Ralph Nader, columnist Molly Ivins and *New York Times* reporter Kurt Eichenwald. The show got big ratings, beating CNN, and didn't include any RRs to outshout Molly.

Later, we did a special in Flint, Michigan, with Michael Moore on violence, guns and racism in connection with his hometown premiere of *Bowling for Columbine*.

Phil hosts Barbara Ehrenreich.

On Labor Day, we aired a powerful one-on-one interview with *Nickel and Dimed* author Barbara Ehrenreich, about trying to survive at low-wage jobs—supplemented by video profiles of a waitress and a home healthcare worker. There was no shouting, no RR, and we beat CNN in viewers, one of the last times that happened.

Another special featured a show-length interview with legendary author and Chicago radio host Studs Terkel; Phil and Studs wore matching red-and-white check shirts and matching red socks (with Phil imitating his guest's fashion sense). That show got poor ratings but was rich television.

We garnered strong ratings when we featured investigative journalists like Rick MacArthur of *Harper's*, who exposed war propaganda and hoaxes—and Greg Palast of the BBC, who discussed the purge of African Americans from Florida voting rolls prior to the 2000 election.

*Donahue* aired various segments challenging the drug war—threats to privacy, racism in enforcement, incarceration of pot smokers—featuring persuasive drug decriminalization advocates like New Mexico governor Gary Johnson, a Republican. We looked at church-state controversies and the power of religious conservatives, with Phil unafraid to speak out for the rights of the non-religious among us.

★  ★  ★

We offered path-breaking coverage of the Israeli-Palestinian conflict. One segment featured teenagers from Seeds of Peace, a camp that brings together Arab and Israeli youths in a forum that emphasizes mutual respect, friendship and ways to transcend prejudice. Another show focused on a husband and wife—Brooklyn-born Jew Adam Shapiro and Detroit-born Palestinian Huwaida Arraf—who met at Seeds of Peace. Phil interviewed them about their peace activism in the Israeli-occupied West Bank and aired revealing footage shot by the two near Ramallah.

We also featured two heartfelt discussions (not acrid debates) involving Jewish fathers whose kids were killed in Israel by Palestinians. One dad was hawkish, the other dovish, both eloquent. The dove was Yitzhak Frankenthal, the Israeli founder of Parents Circle, a peace initiative by Israeli and Palestinian parents who'd lost children in the conflict. Phil quoted from a speech Frankenthal made outside the home of Israel's prime minister:

My beloved son, my own flesh and blood, was murdered by Palestinians. My tall, blue-eyed, golden-haired son, who was always smiling with the innocence of a child and the understanding of an adult. My son. If to hit his killers, innocent Palestinian children and other civilians would have to be killed, I would ask the security forces to wait for another opportunity. If the security forces were to kill innocent Palestinians as well, I would tell them they were no better than my son's killers.

In our third week on the air, amid escalating Palestinian and Israeli attacks, Phil interviewed Shimon Peres, then Israel's foreign minister in a coalition government with conservative prime minister Ariel Sharon. Phil noted that Peres had criticized a recent Israeli missile assault in Gaza City that had killed a Hamas leader and nine innocent children, wounding dozens—but Phil reacted loudly when Peres seemed to euphemize the attack:

PERES: Unfortunately, in every war, you have mistakes. The greatest mistake is war itself.

DONAHUE: That was an F-16. It was an apartment building. . . . That is *not* a mistake—to fire a missile into an apartment building at midnight. What, this terrorist is the only guy sleeping in that building? It is not a mistake. It was a direct action that you knew would cause civilian deaths.*

Peres appeared startled by Phil's response. Israeli officials are used to strong questioning from Israeli reporters, but rarely from American journalists.

In his unique style, Phil praised Peres on his Nobel Peace Prize for negotiating the 1993 Oslo accords with Yasser Arafat: "What a wonderful, wonderful honor. What mother wouldn't want her son—the Nobel Prize?" Then Phil asked about some rarely mentioned history: "Since Oslo, we've had a doubling of Israeli settlers. Now how is there possibly light at the end of this tunnel?"

Eight days later, Phil interviewed former Israeli prime minister Ehud Barak. (I was surprised no one had warned Barak away from Phil in the intervening days.) Phil asked Barak if the expansion of Israeli settlements on Palestinian land was a "territorial grab" undermining "the peace process." He also posed a question rarely asked in U.S. media: whether Barak's famous offer—rejected by Arafat at Camp

---

*In the interest of full disclosure, MSNBC's corporate parent builds engines for the F-16 fighter aircraft.

David in 2000—had been all that "generous" if it divided the Palestinian state into "chunks, with Israeli settlements in between . . . a balkanization" of their homeland.

Phil followed his Barak segment with an interview of Palestinian leader Hanan Ashrawi, to whom he also posed hard questions: "Ms. Ashrawi, 75 Palestinian suicide bombing attacks since September of 2000—Jewish teenagers waiting to get into a disco, a seder dinner, innocent people celebrating. You know, I don't see the outrage from Arafat. I don't see the outrage from the Palestinian people. I see Palestinians jumping up and down with joy."

I worked closely with Phil on these shows. He knew he would catch heat for toughly questioning Israeli leaders, but he was steadfast. His courage was impressive.

At MSNBC and elsewhere, I met several network TV journalists with long experience in the Middle East who told me of fears about sending home news that cast Israel in a bad light. Correspondents learned that accuracy and evenhandedness meant less to network higher-ups than avoiding conflict with organized "Israel-right-or-wrong" lobbies.

★  ★  ★

The impending war with Iraq was our signature issue. We launched *Donahue* with a debate on Iraq, and followed with many more, even

after management said we were overdoing the story. Some segments turned into shoutfests that did not allow for clear rebuttal of prewar fabrications—but our program consistently featured the foremost critics of the Iraq adventure, such as Congressmen Dennis Kucinich and Bernie Sanders, Phyllis Bennis of the Institute for Policy Studies and Ambassador Edward Peck, former U.S. chief of mission in Iraq.

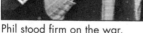

Phil stood firm on the war.

*Donahue* continued to book Scott Ritter in the face of smears that he was a paid Saddamite agent.

In August 2002, I was a *Donahue* panelist in an Iraq debate with Rich Lowry, the *National Review* editor whose zeal for military action was impairing his analysis. He asserted that Saddam was "seeking nuclear weapons." Strike 1. That "the Iraqis will celebrate" a U.S. invasion. Strike 2. And that after Saddam was removed, the United States was "going to pour in a massive amount of aid." Strike 3.

I explained global opposition to an American invasion by noting that the United States had overthrown elected governments from Iran to Chile, ushering in despotic regimes: "When out of Washington we're going to change another regime, the conservatives dance in this country. But around the world they shudder—because the history of U.S. foreign policy is regime change that often makes things worse."

Another panelist in the discussion was rightwinger Bay Buchanan (Patrick's sister), who warned that a U.S. attack on Iraq would destabilize the Middle East.

LOWRY: You know, that region should be destabilized. There are three regimes that should be destabilized out of existence: Iran, Iraq and Syria. And another regime, Saudi Arabia, that needs drastic changing. And the only way you're going to do it is to have massive assertions of U.S. power in the region.

BUCHANAN: Richard, are you proposing a four-front war?

(CROSSTALK)

COHEN: . . . with the cowboys in the Bush administration, you'll have more enemies in the world than friends.

LOWRY: Three thousand people died.

Like clockwork, I heard that non sequitur response—"3,000 people have died"—whenever I questioned the wisdom of invading Iraq. Echoing through talk TV and radio, the refrain helped confuse half the country into believing that Saddam was involved in Sept. 11.

★ ★ ★

There were many extraordinary moments on *Donahue*. But they were too sporadic—and sometimes sandwiched between a futile shouting match for "balance" and a celebrity interview or crime story update. You can't be hit-or-miss and expect to build a loyal niche audience in cable news. You need consistency, and time. We had neither.

O'Reilly's slow, steady climb to well beyond a million viewers would have been impossible if he'd zigzagged in viewpoint and tone from segment to segment and night to night—sometimes offering a loud clear conservative message, and sometimes not. I monitored viewer emails to our show from the beginning; our inconsistency was driving away our base, the kind of activist-oriented, email-connected viewers who would have helped spread the word.

During the same months that *Donahue* had its shaky foothold on national TV but was not allowed to offer a coherent viewpoint, other media endeavors on the left were booming—thanks to clear opposition to Bush and the approaching war. These projects weren't under the thumb of MSNBC brass. Indeed, they flourished as alternatives to what MSNBC and corporate media were offering. Websites like CommonDreams and blogs like *DailyKos* were exploding, as was *Democracy Now!* on radio and TV. Membership in the online organization MoveOn.org was going through the roof, beyond a million U.S. activists. I later asked MoveOn's Eli Pariser if it was true that his group doubled its membership over the war issue. "No," he said. "We tripled our membership."

## RATINGS AND FOCUS GROUPS

Thanks to prelaunch media buzz, MSNBC had accomplished a miracle on the opening night of *Donahue*: The channel finally beat CNN in the ratings. Not by a lot (roughly a million viewers vs. 800,000), but enough for MSNBC to crow about in a release to TV writers. *Donahue* beat CNN on the next two nights, just barely—but enough for MSNBC to issue two more releases on its ratings victories. It struck some of us at *Donahue* as an unseemly display from a management team that had been in last place for a loooong time.

Day 3 was one of the last times *Donahue* (or any MSNBC primetime show) beat CNN. Management hadn't thought that far in advance . . . three days. In no time, TV writers—perhaps noticing that no releases were forthcoming from MSNBC and prodded by CNN—pounced on the story that *Donahue*'s ratings were falling, and fixated on it for months.

A smarter PR approach for MSNBC in the opening days, since artificially-inflated ratings can't sustain in cable news, would have been to emphasize *Donahue*'s unique topics and guests. I worried that MSNBC brass were ungrounded enough to actually believe *Donahue* could open with a million viewers and maintain that audience. A year before our debut, MSNBC—then in its sixth year—averaged less than 250,000 viewers in our timeslot.

Almost as important to TV executives as their total audience is the number of viewers in the 25-to-54 age demographic that advertisers cherish. This group is known in TV Land as "The Demo." It was sometimes difficult to assess the Demo—because of the small numbers MSNBC was accustomed to. Our show featuring 90-year-old Studs Terkel got good buzz from viewers, but the Demo was too small to measure. (Studs' red-check shirt and red socks didn't grab the pregray crowd.) After shows on which our Demo number beat meager overall ratings, it was common to hear a *Donahue* producer offer upbeat spin: "Well, we didn't do too bad in the Demo."

In law school, I learned: If you have the facts on your side, pound the facts. If you have the law on your side, pound the law. If you have neither, pound the table. At MSNBC, when necessary, we'd pound the Demo.

★ ★ ★

In September 2002, in an effort to boost our ratings, I worked with MSNBC's ad department to develop a "big bang for little bucks" *Donahue* ad campaign in progressive magazines. Long overdue, it would be a tiny expenditure compared with that spent on prelaunch advertising. I compiled a list of publications; the ad department put together a budget—just $60,000. But then, nothing happened. After several days, I approached one of the heads of the department: "That ad campaign is off," he told me, matter-of-factly. "We're reframing the show."

Reframing the show? We'd been on the air only two months, two *summer* months. I was a *Donahue* "senior producer" and had to hear this from the ad guy! "Reframing" meant less issues, more tabloid, more celebs. I apparently heard the news before Phil.

Instead of an ad campaign aimed at an easily-reached audience hungry for a progressive voice on TV, MSNBC was launching a fall marketing effort for *Donahue* aimed at the broad populace—a mini-rerun of the futile summer ad campaign.

I exchanged emails with a top MSNBC executive. It convinced me that MSNBC was too clueless (or too constrained by GE ownership/ NBC management) to succeed in cable news. I was told that *Donahue* ads in progressive magazines might conflict with MSNBC's slogan: "fiercely independent." Even goofier, I was told that their new pitch would be aimed at getting "moderate and/or apolitical viewers (especially women) to jump on the *Donahue* bandwagon. . . . To get elected, we need to attract (or at least not drive away) the 'middle'—so my limited advertising funds are going to be directed at them."

This struck me as beyond foolish, but my return email was diplomatic:

> To get elected—more akin to broadcasting—one needs the middle of the road and a majority of voters. In narrowcasting, where you can win with a million viewers, the "Fair and Balanced" network showed the value of audience-building through targeted ads on rightwing talk radio. Enticing sympathetic or open-minded news-oriented types to *Donahue* seems easier and cheaper than bringing apolitical folks to cable news.

I got no response. The Suits continued to prohibit ads to our natural audience while wondering why *Donahue* wasn't doing better in the ratings.

★ ★ ★

It was around this time I started hearing about focus groups. Things were getting sillier as management was getting more panicked. Plain folks had been assembled and probed for their reaction to the show. The verdict was in: Phil had to be "less opinionated, less combative, more patriotic." The show was "too strident." The bosses wanted me to carry the message to Phil: "Talk to him, Jeff. He'll listen to you."

I refused. They were in full gallop down the wrong path that began with a massive ad campaign aimed at no one specific, just Middle America. For *Donahue* to succeed, it couldn't be aimed at, or calibrated for, "moderate apolitical" folks. If Fox had tested O'Reilly and his nasty on-air antics on mainstream focus groups, he would have been off the air years ago. Yet he came to dominate cable news, because of his appeal largely to an audience of likeminded politicized viewers.

Our show could have benefited from a focus group—if the group was assembled from the millions of members of MoveOn, NOW, Sierra Club and People for the American Way. Or from the tens of millions who, in polls, are self-described "liberals." Over time, a program tailored to *and advertised to* that audience would have prospered.

## PINCH-HITTING IN PRIMETIME

In the Superman legend, after a quick change of clothes, a mild-mannered journalist morphs into a superhero. I'm no hero, but sometimes I'd be called on to save the day by filling in for a scheduled *Donahue* guest who had to cancel right before airtime. It was an odd role; most news shows don't have senior producers on standby who double as on-air pundits.

A couple times, I frustrated my colleagues by saying no—my refusal based on the quaint idea that commentators should actually know a certain amount about the topic on which they're pontificating. Other times, I allowed myself to be used as a pinch-hitter, sometimes without time even for practice swings.

One night we opened the show with a weird crime story: two brothers, aged 12 and 13, had been convicted that day in Florida of killing their dad. After confessing to the killing, the brothers had changed their story, saying the real killer was a 40-year-old neighbor who'd molested one of the boys and intimidated them into confessing. I hadn't become a news analyst to be debating this type of story. But our star guest, our "big get"—lawyer-pundit Mickey Sherman, the attorney for Kennedy cousin Michael Skakel—was stuck in traffic and couldn't do the show.

I had only minutes to prepare. Beyond trying two kids as adults, what made this case thoroughly strange was that the prosecutor had simultaneously tried the 40-year-old child molester for the same murder—arguing before one jury that he was the killer and the boys were telling the truth, while arguing before another jury that the boys were liars and murderers. It was this latter jury that had convicted the boys.

No one could accuse me of overpreparing for this debate. Maybe it was the little time I had that helped me focus my comments on the essence of the story—the prosecution's outrageous conduct: "I have that old-fashioned notion that a prosecutor should investigate the crime, figure out what happened and then prosecute someone. You don't guess. Because, Phil, in one of the cases he's putting on something that he knows is a lie."

My lack of depth on the case didn't prevent me from emoting—"American justice has just been shredded in Florida. . . . I don't hear any outrage." I seemed to be channeling the insufferable Nancy Grace, the tabloid bloviater on CNN and Court TV.*

★  ★  ★

Following the Florida murder discussion, Phil interviewed conservative icon Ollie North in a spirited yet friendly debate on Iraq—during which North claimed that Bush had proof of Iraqi WMD and that European countries were helping Iraq build WMD. North clearly enjoyed the interview; his book was repeatedly plugged; he vowed to return to the show. But a rightwing viewer complained in an error-filled email that North had been mistreated: "Phil Donahue has such a smug, contemptuous attitude towards Republicans."

It was clear our show was in trouble when a top MSNBC executive asked me to comment on this shrill complaint from a viewer not even close to our target audience. The fear was that we were offending conservatives. The exec never asked me about the many dozens of progressive viewers who'd sent thoughtful emails explaining why they were abandoning our show. Days later, I was told of *Donahue* being "reframed" away from political issues.

★  ★  ★

In September, I was rushed into emergency duty again—this time on one of my strongest subjects: the White House push for war in Iraq. I had little time to collect my thoughts before dashing on the air in place of Congressman Jesse Jackson Jr., who was stuck at an airport. I joined my friend and *Nation* correspondent John Nichols in a lengthy, raucous debate with former Republican strategist Peter Roff and GOP operative Ed Gillespie, who became Republican Party chair months later.

Nichols and I had the home-court advantage in the *Donahue* studio in New Jersey; they appeared by remote from Washington. We were on the offensive from the start, questioning the timing of the Iraq war push, while the GOP side claimed that charges about the war drive being politically motivated were "reprehensible" and "outrageous." I can't remember seeing such a show—let alone participating in one—

---

*Weeks later, the trial judge overturned the boys' convictions, saying the prosecutor's "unusual and bizarre" decision to try another man for the same killing violated their due process rights.

where we not only debunked Republican spin but at times were laughing at it.

With Nichols in the lead and Phil backing us, we argued that the White House was using war as an electoral weapon. To win congressional elections, Bush political advisor Karl Rove had instructed Republicans to focus voters' attention on war and "national security." Team Bush had waited until September 2002 to

Rare TV moment in 2002: GOP side on the defensive

demand a speedy, preelection vote in Congress on war with Iraq. Asked about the rushed timing, the White House chief of staff had said, "From a marketing point of view, you don't introduce new products in August." The "new product" was WAR.

Nichols declared, "Karl Rove has said all year to us, he has said, 'Look, this election's got to be about national security.' Now we're 45 days from the election, and what's the issue we're talking about?"

Gillespie replied:

> It is reprehensible to suggest that the timing of the debate over Iraq and our decision toward Iraq is timed toward the election. And in fact, it would be more reprehensible to suggest that we should move it back past the election 'til the next Congress, when there is information out there that says that this man, Saddam Hussein, is acquiring the possibility of having biochemical weapons of mass destruction, nuclear weapons.

After a break, Phil noted Ed Gillespie's leading role in "the Republican revolution" and summed up the discussion: "You were breathless with indignation that these guests gathered here with me would suggest that somehow the president's war on Iraq is intended to divert from Halliburton, Harken, Enron, WorldCom." Soon after, Nichols piped in, "What Ed is indignant about, and what is so reprehensible is that we're actually sitting here talking about the reality of politics, not about what's in the spin."

I repeatedly questioned the timing of the congressional debate on the Iraq war resolution:

The Bush administration here is proposing, trying to sell, a massive war. This isn't Grenada. It's not Panama. It's a massive war. And they're saying that Congress has got to discuss it in the next two weeks. Now, if you don't think that's politically motivated—if this president was really concerned about a real debate . . . they'd say, Let's continue this debate after the election, where we can really have a full discussion.

★  ★  ★

I got more positive viewer-feedback on that appearance than any other on MSNBC. Advocates on our side held the offensive in a way that O'Reilly does each night for the other side. It was the kind of show that, if done consistently, would have built audience.

It was also the kind of show that made management tremble—the kind that management was committed to terminating. We would learn later of an internal NBC memo that damned Phil because "he seems to delight in presenting guests who are antiwar, anti-Bush and skeptical of the administration's motives."

The NBC memo was illuminating about the limits of debate: Mainstream media allow dissent about war—but usually only on tactics, *not motives*. It's acceptable to critique the Iraq war as ill-planned or ill-executed, but not to suggest that the war was less about freedom and democracy than about politics or empire or military bases or oil. When Congressman Kucinich suggested oil as a major motivation for the Iraq war, quasi-liberal *Washington Post* columnist Richard Cohen fumed, "How did this fool get on *Meet the Press*?"

★  ★  ★

I made my last *Donahue* appearance as a "week in review" panelist before Thanksgiving 2002—discussing everything from Michael Jackson's parenting follies to lawsuits against McDonald's. But I went totally speechless when an attractive news anchorwoman from Toronto joined the panel. I had trouble focusing on the words she was saying. This had never happened to me before. But then I'd never appeared before with an anchor from Naked News, known for disrobing during each of her newscasts.

# THE GET

In TV news, everyone from the network boss to the top talent to the intern is a booker, trying to recruit the most famous and timely guest possible—the "get." For the *Donahue* premiere, I'd "efforted" Springsteen without success. Since I had connections to some actors and musicians through my years at FAIR, I was sometimes enlisted as a *Donahue* celebrity booker. I was happy to do it since the celebs I knew were all socially-conscious with plenty to say—a vast improvement over guests like Dr. Phil or Regis Philbin.

In October 2002, singer-activist Harry Belafonte made controversial comments on a radio show likening Secretary of State Colin Powell to a house slave in Bush's White House, who remains privileged only "as long as he will serve the master." The remarks provoked an angry response from Powell. For days, Belafonte was one of the most talked-about figures in the news, but he had not gone public to explain his comments.

Like almost every other TV news producer in the land, I was asked to "effort" Belafonte. Using my progressive connections and working with a super-aggressive fellow producer, we persuaded the Belafonte camp to have him break his silence on *Donahue.* There was obviously goodwill toward Phil from Belafonte—this was something of a favor to us and our struggling show. It would be a huge "get."

To firm up the booking, all we had to do on our end was postpone a prescheduled interview with NBC's Tim Russert and quickly get back to Belafonte's people. As the host of *Meet the Press*, Russert would clearly understand Belafonte's news value and timeliness. But to my horror, the Suits decided inexplicably to stay with Russert.

Our big "get". . . days late

The decision was so boneheaded, I wondered if management was unconsciously trying to sabotage *Donahue.* Belafonte would have generated positive buzz. Our big get had gotten away.

Later, in agony and self-torture, I turned on Larry King to see him open his CNN show: "Tonight, exclusive—what's Harry Belafonte's problem with Colin Powell? He's here to explain his controversial remarks about the secretary of state."

Two days after appearing on Larry King, Belafonte made a powerful appearance on *Donahue*—with almost no buzz before or after. Few cared. We were like the second man to walk on the moon.

★  ★  ★

Since I knew Susan Sarandon and Tim Robbins from their stalwart support of FAIR, I was asked from the beginning of *Donahue* if I could book them—as a couple. It was a nice idea, a show I'd want to watch. But while the two artist-activists had made movies and raised a family together, they didn't usually appear together on TV chat shows. Nevertheless, as a team player, I started *efforting* the couple.

For months their schedules didn't permit any appearances. Unfortunately, by the time they said yes, and yes to a rare joint appearance, it was December; the Suits had largely seized control of *Donahue* and were turning it into a Fox News look-alike. So Sarandon and Robbins appeared on a show framed heavily on the question "Is being antiwar un-American?" They were joined on stage—actually preceded on stage—by a bitter fellow who'd written a screed called *Why the Left Hates America* and who repeatedly mischaracterized their views.

The two actors were quite strong under the circumstances, forcefully questioning the rush to invade Iraq and criticizing the corporate media for prowar bias. In his opening comment, Robbins eloquently challenged the notion that dissent is un-American:

> Blind support for leaders isn't the domain of a democracy. It's more the domain of a communist dictatorship. The great thing about America is we can ask questions, and the leaders work for us. We elect them. And so they're responsible to us. We're not responsible to them.

During a commercial break, it was learned that the left-bashing author *himself* was antiwar on the issue of invading Iraq. The rightwinger was outed in the next segment. Pressed by Phil on why he opposed a war with Iraq, the author sheepishly said, "The bottom line is that to conflate Saddam Hussein with Bin Laden is kind of foolish."

It's too bad that conservatives who doubted the war weren't as vocal in expressing their doubts as in questioning the patriotism of others.

★ ★ ★

The day after this show, a fuming email was sent to NBC chief Bob Wright by a rightwing business consultant who seemed to imply he was an acquaintance of Wright's. The "Dear Bob" email—cc'd to MSNBC's president—griped that Phil Donahue had spent years deceptively promoting "his anti-American, anti-Christian, pro-perversion philosophy" and that *Donahue* lacked "fair and balanced discussion":

> I would expect a responsible and prestigious news network like NBC to "police" this kind of primetime, irresponsible programming and hosting. . . . You do a great disservice to this country and to its citizenry by letting this kind of unbalanced deception continue on primetime, during your watch.

A responsible news network wouldn't have been bothered by an emailer railing against a host's alleged anti-Americanism. But at MSNBC, the email bounced through management like a neutron in a GE nuclear reactor—taken seriously because it reinforced management's conformist fears and biases.

By this time, *Donahue* had provoked informed criticism from hundreds of progressive viewers who complained that the show was deteriorating . . . was favoring conservative loudmouths . . . was imitating Fox. Many had protested repeatedly before turning the show off for good. To MSNBC management, the diatribe from a single cranky businessman mattered more than the multitude of criticisms from our base.

Earth to Suitville: Rightwing businessmen are not in our prime Demo.

# CHAPTER NINE
## *DONAHUE* CRASHES

In November 2002, management essentially seized control of *Donahue* in a quiet coup. What happened during the last months of the show can't be blamed on its dedicated staff or on Phil. The downward spiral was engineered in Suitville.

From the beginning, management's dictates had shaped and misshaped *Donahue*. But the orders had come from afar—and could sometimes be resisted or evaded by staff. Now the Suits took over day-to-day control. Resistance was next to impossible.

The only change that wasn't completely foolish was to put *Donahue* in front of a live studio audience at 30 Rockefeller Center in New York (where Phil had ruled the roost a decade earlier). The audience involvement, with Phil scurrying up and down the aisles like in the old days, added sparks to the show . . . along with a bunch of new expenses.

Management's next changes were just plain dumb—changes that doomed the show and prevented it from seeing the clear ratings boost that a studio-audience program should have delivered. The overriding directive was to slant the show rightward. In essence, the plan was to imitate Fox News—and, as time went on, to try to outfox Fox.

The new order at *Donahue* evoked comedian Fred Allen, who once said that the minds that control television "are so small you could put them in the navel of a flea and still have room beside them for a network vice president's heart."*

---

*It's worth noting that, despite the Suits' mismanagement, *Donahue* remained MSNBC's most watched show.

In December, one management dictate became near sacred. It was stated and re-stated to everyone on staff, and producers who did not fulfill the mandate were chewed out by management: Debates on political topics had to be *imbalanced*. You read that right: *not* balanced. If we booked one guest who was antiwar on Iraq, we needed two who were prowar. If we booked two guests on the left, we needed three on the right. At one staff meeting, a producer proposed booking Michael Moore and was told she'd need *three* rightwingers for balance.

I thought about proposing Noam Chomsky as a guest, but our stage couldn't accommodate the 23 rightwingers we would have needed for balance.

The tilt-right order was beyond strange, for a few reasons:

1. Since before *Donahue* launched, we'd been told by management—without explanation—that the key to our show's success was strict balance. Now, we were told *imbalance* was the key to success.

2. You can't outfox Fox for ratings—they own the franchise and audience for rightwing cable news.

3. You certainly can't outfox Fox when your host is the most famous liberal on TV. If viewers are hankering for a show dominated by conservative voices, why watch Phil Donahue?

MSNBC's strategy of competing for Fox's viewers became clearer weeks later with the hiring of a couple rightwing hosts. The Suits were trapped by their self-fulfilling dogma that cable news audiences are immutably conservative. The idea of reaching out to new audiences—those tired of Fox and its copycats—with a progressive show was too wildly subversive for a GE-owned/NBC-run network.

When *Donahue* producers asked for reasoning behind the right-tilting guest list, the Suits wouldn't come clean about their Foxization strategy. They half-heartedly argued that since Phil is a liberal, he should be counted as a left advocate in calculating right-left balance. The problem was that—besides Phil's attention being diverted to intros, outros, phone calls, emails, studio audience and refereeing duties—he'd been pressured for months by management to tone it down and be less partisan.

There was another problem. When we arrived at MSNBC, right-winger Alan Keyes hosted a show, but his guest list didn't favor the left to achieve some sort of balance. When we departed MSNBC, rightwinger Joe Scarborough hosted a show, but his guest list didn't favor the left.

As everyone knew, this was a network policy aimed at one and only one host: Phil Donahue.

## DON'T QUESTION AUTHORITY

A nagging irritation to management from the start of *Donahue* was that Phil's questioning of authority figures was deemed "too angry." He didn't show due deference in one-on-one interviews. The complaint was that Phil "badgered" powerful guests when he didn't accept their answers or evasions. The reality is that while Phil could pose hard questions, he was almost always polite and good-natured—not rude or disrespectful like other cable news hosts.

Clearly, Phil was unintimidated by the powerful. He could be tenacious with those he called "laptop bombers" pushing for war in Iraq: *Where's the evidence? Why the rush? Where's the media? Where's Congress?* Whether questioning officials or elite journalists, he was holding those in power accountable—which is what journalism is supposed to do.

Management saw it differently. They were anxious over how Phil interviewed TV news heavyweights like Tim Russert and Ted Koppel, and they feared that such guests would not return. ("Who the hell cares," I wrote at the time, "whether Koppel returns or not?") Concerns were also raised about how Phil interviewed Israeli leaders and others.

The relentless pressure and scrutiny from MSNBC brass sometimes affected Phil on-air. His strength has been his emotional connection to audiences, his passion, his ability to take issues mainstream. He wasn't always the best counterpuncher in debates, and now the Suits were wrongheadedly urging him to pull his punches. Given the contradictory orders and stress he was under, I marveled at how well he performed night after night.

The effort to tone Phil down was yet another worry in Suitville deriving more from their own discomforts and biases than from any consideration of audience-building. Down the block, O'Reilly was amassing quite a crowd by being anything but toned down.

Along with the fear that Phil was too tough on establishment guests was the insistence that he be tougher on progressive guests and ask them devil's advocate questions: "Help keep him honest," I was emailed by a top exec, "with those he's inclined to agree with." Ailes would have cackled at such advice.

Since it was part of my job, at least at the beginning, to brief Phil about possible questions to ask guests, I was often blamed for Phil's "badgering." In later months, if the topic or guest were deemed delicate, I was instructed not to communicate with Phil at all.

The issue of tough questioning of guests became more acute after management demanded that rightwingers dominate our guest list. Weeks before the war, with *Donahue* offering yet another debate in which the antiwar side was to be outnumbered, I was told not to talk to Phil about points he might raise. That day, in an angry "memo to self," I wrote, "When we were more balanced, there was worry about my communications with Phil. He might ask tough questions of folks in power, might impart a progressive orientation."

Now Phil was outnumbered: "So we have an outgunned host I'm not supposed to help. This place is outflanking Fox News on the right. Management here is not just a problem of too many chefs in the kitchen, but too many and not one who can cook. They know neither how to do real news, nor how to attract an audience with faux news. At least Fox knows how to do the latter."

★  ★  ★

MSNBC's fair-haired boy

Despite lackluster ratings, Chris Matthews was literally MSNBC's fair-haired boy—baby-faced, motor-mouthed, with that shock of blond hair. To me, Matthews resembled a barroom drunk who talks louder (and faster) the less he knows about a subject. His inside-the-Beltway show *Hardball* is usually soft on officialdom, long on the conventional, and short on wisdom.

At Fox News back in 2000, I remember Bill O'Reilly telling me in a greenroom that he was beating *Hardball* (then at CNBC) in viewership—and grousing that Matthews got attention and guests beyond what his ratings warranted. I didn't argue with him. Beltway insiders seem to like Matthews more than the masses of viewers.

A former Democratic operative who grew conservative, he became a featured speaker at gatherings of corporate interest groups. Matthews has often expressed an elite contempt for the have-nots: "The big fight in this country," he once declared, "is between the people who don't work on welfare and the people who do."

It's obvious that Phil's arrival at MSNBC created the same anxiety for Matthews as for the Suits. *Donahue* had been on the air 10 weeks when a *U.S. News & World Report* gossip item in October 2002 told of an unprovoked Matthews outburst against his MSNBC teammate:

Feasting at Washington's La Colline last week . . . Matthews let loose on old Phil. A lunch partner says Matthews complained that Donahue focuses too much on what's wrong with America. "That," he's quoted saying, "is the wrong face for MSNBC." Matthews predicted that if Donahue stays on the air, he could bring down the network.

Phil was charitable about the slur and let it pass. He had little choice, since what Matthews was saying at fancy D.C. eateries is exactly what the Suits were saying internally, as they went about reshaping our show.

One day before the November 2002 elections, Phil graciously hosted Matthews on *Donahue* to discuss congressional races and a new book Matthews was plugging. The live face-to-face interview was to be a few segments, but it turned into a train wreck that consumed the whole show (bumping an interview with actor Ray Romano). Once it got heated, Matthews called it "the Irish fight card." The show began slowly and warmly with Matthews rightfully pointing out that he, not just Phil, questioned the wisdom of invading Iraq. But it boiled into a tense confrontation as a result of Matthews' pent-up need to distinguish himself from Phil; there was a patriotic way to challenge the war—his way—and an un-American way: Phil's way.

Matthews felt compelled to repeatedly insist, contrary to evidence, that war in Iraq would be a departure from our country's history as a "reluctant warrior"—part of his fanciful theory that Americans are heroic misfits who save the world only when asked.*

Matthews was intent on separating himself from Phil:

> I really do think we have a different attitude about the world and this country. I think you are a very good critic of this country. . . . You're like Michael Moore. You find all the things that's wrong with us. You're excellent about the corporate deal-making and the failure to protect blue-collar jobs and all that. . . . The glass is always half-empty to you. It's always half-empty. You're always negative, and I think that's a problem. I disagree with that point of view. I think this is the greatest country in the world, with some flaws.

Phil reacted by accusing Matthews and "Beltway boys" in the press corps of being too cozy with the powerful—and that his hidden message was: "Stop complaining! Shut up, shut up, shut up." Phil said he felt "blessed to be an American" and waxed poetic about our Constitution ("a magnificent work of art") and the Bill of Rights ("defending the individual against the power of the state") and privacy rights ("this is a great nation that refuses to say all women who are pregnant shall remain pregnant by order of the state").

But Matthews wasn't buying it. He seemed to want the world to know that he was the one patriot at the table.**

------

*A day after the debate, I wrote a response to Matthews' claim that the U.S. has been a "reluctant warrior" historically: "Since 1945, the U.S. has invaded or intervened militarily in many countries, including the Philippines (late '40s), Lebanon ('58), Haiti ('59), Vietnam, Cambodia and Laos ('60s–'70s), Peru ('65), Dominican Republic ('65), Grenada ('83), Libya ('86), Panama ('89), Iraq ('91), Somalia ('93), Yugoslavia ('99), Colombia ('90s–present). In almost all cases, these countries had not attacked the U.S. or any neighbor. The U.S. has covertly intervened to overthrow a democratic government and/or impose a military dictatorship in Iran ('53), Guatemala ('54), Brazil ('64), Indonesia ('65), Greece ('67) and Chile ('73). The U.S. military has bases in dozens of foreign countries. Our military budget of nearly $400 billion is larger than the military budgets of the next 25 countries combined." Given our fragile position at MSNBC, it was decided not to post my rebuttal on the *Donahue* webpage.

**After the invasion of Iraq, Matthews rushed to duck and cover behind Bush, in often embarrassing fashion. When U.S. troops seized Baghdad, he proclaimed, "We are all neo-cons now," and asked, "Why don't the damn Democrats give the

The morning after the Phil-Matthews brawl, Don Imus re-aired some of it on his MSNBC/radio simulcast: "Good for Chris Matthews," enthused Imus. "He's got some *cojones*, doesn't he?" After airing a segment in which Phil defended a woman's right to choose, Imus went after him on abortion: "It's not a means of birth control. Get over it. That's just ridiculous. Any woman who thinks she has a right to choose to kill babies is a moron. And they should be prosecuted."

Phil was feeling as welcome at MSNBC as a feminist at Augusta National Golf Club.

## VIRGINS DON'T NEED ABORTIONS

In December 2002, under management's firm command, *Donahue* marched onward and rightward. Instead of comprehensive interviews with Barbara Ehrenreich or Michael Moore, we now featured a show-length interview with Jerry Falwell. A debate on gender equality—headlined "Are Women Getting a Free Ride?"—pitted one feminist against several antifeminists. It was teased, "Are women getting a free pass from divorce court to the workplace? Do equal rights give women a leg up on men in America?"

The conservative turn didn't boost ratings. In fact, the most watched show of the month was a Dec. 5 debate on the backlash of "Angry White Men" against affirmative action, immigration and feminism—with a guest list that did *not* favor conservatives. The right-tilt order was not yet fully in place. On the starboard side were Pat Buchanan and a former Republican congressman. On the other side were civil rights advocate Ron Daniels, feminist Gloria Allred and Dave Chappelle. Yes, *that* Chappelle, the racially conscious comic ("I'm Rick James, bitch!") from Comedy Central. I was at the studio for this show. Chappelle didn't say much—but he giggled a lot and seemed to thoroughly enjoy the experience, even when he referred to Pat Buchanan as Pat Robertson. That night I was glad MSNBC wasn't drug-testing its guests.

---

president his day?" When Bush declared "Mission Accomplished" in Iraq, Matthews gushed at length about his looks and authenticity: "We're proud of our president. Americans love having a *guy* as president, a guy who has a little swagger. . . . We like having a hero as president. We're not like the Brits." And he calls this *Hardball*.

Drug charges and hallucinations were bandied about a few days later on a hawk-heavy show on Iraq. It featured former weapons inspector Bill Tierney—who asserted that "Iraq has nuclear weapons, folks. You'd better sober up to the reality"—and obsessive Iraq "expert" Laurie Mylroie, asserting that Saddam was behind Sept. 11. In response, a dovish guest said she was paranoid and saw Saddam behind all things bad in our country, including "male-pattern baldness." He continued: "Take your medication now, Dr. Mylroie."

On Dec. 12, the day of the *Washington Post* fable about Iraq supplying chemical weapons to terrorists, a *Donahue* debate on Iraq pitted two ultra-hawks against the authoritative but outnumbered William Hartung of the World Policy Institute. The show was dominated by Ken Adelman, who famously predicted that war with Iraq would be a "cakewalk." A look back at the transcript reveals that Hartung's cautious comments about invading Iraq and the *Post* story ("I think this was leaked to fuel the fire for war") stand up well to history. But his words were hardly audible at the time, when it mattered. I apologized to Hartung after the show—which would become a common practice for me.

With prowar guests predominant on *Donahue* and shows framed with headlines such as "Are antiwar activists unpatriotic?" it was dissent—not a war based on deceit—that was too often on the defensive.

★  ★  ★

*Donahue* began 2003 in a full-throttle effort to outfox Fox News. And the ratings suffered.

So did my role on the show. It was hard for me in good conscience to book progressive guests, since our forum was often less friendly than O'Reilly's—with one-fifth the viewers. (Progressive slots were shrinking anyway, due to our affirmative action quota system for rightists.) My briefing role was also reduced, as higher-ups grew uncomfortable with me discussing possible talking points with Phil. In pursuit of a Fox audience, it seemed that management's goal was to have Phil's side lose.

My one remaining task on the show was to write the "Daily Donahue" promo email sent to our list. It wasn't easy generating enthusiasm for the programs we were offering, such as a panel pitting one pro-choice guest against three advocates of outlawing abortion. Or a show on abstinence-only education. In writing the emails, I tried at least to keep myself amused. Here's an example:

Teen sex and the new virginity on tonight's *Donahue*. More and more teens are doing it . . . choosing virginity over sex and publicly declaring that they are abstaining. Is this a new sexual revolution (or counterrevolution)?

Keep the little kiddies away as Phil leads a debate on teaching abstinence-only vs. comprehensive sex education. The Bush administration is steering your tax money to abstinence-only programs.

You can't believe the talk I've had to endure as producers sitting next to me have been preparing tonight's show by interviewing virgins about exactly what is or is not deemed "celibacy." Such talk cannot be repeated on the air. (If I were a prude, I'd have a strong case of sexual harassment—"hostile work environment.")

In the "No One Asked Me Department": Speaking as a parent, if my daughter was marrying someone she'd never had sex with, I'd be worried, not comforted.

That night's "New Virginity" show produced some new lows—including a record for lopsidedness: two sex-ed advocates vs. more than a half-dozen abstinence proponents.

And it produced new lows in ratings. Despite a live studio audience and a bevy of virgins, it was pretty much our tiniest viewership ever. In the 25-to-54 demo, the rating was a zero.

Management was running *Donahue* into the ground. I received two dozen complaints from liberals about the abstinence show—how the sex education side was outnumbered, how *Donahue* was becoming "worse than Fox." I wondered if they were the last remaining liberals still watching.

★ ★ ★

The next night, the record for lopsidedness was broken anew with a show titled "Donahue Takes on the Women of the Right"—no progressive guests, just Phil against four conservative women.

This show sent my mind spinning to the start of *Donahue*, when I was arguing for a show oriented as leftward as O'Reilly's show was rightward—where Phil would crusade on issues he cared about, just like O'Reilly's show, without worrying about balance any more than O'Reilly does. (I never proposed that Phil be as rude or arrogant.)

Over and over, the response I got from higher-ups was "But Phil's not O'Reilly!" This objection proved ironic in the last months of our show. O'Reilly's forte is interrogation of (usually weak) liberals.

Interrogation was not Phil's strongest suit. But management was pushing him into that role—not just that of O'Reilly, but Super-O'Reilly, able to take on a gaggle of conservatives at once.

## ANGRY WHITE MEN

Having blocked a progressive-oriented *Donahue* from day 1, management was now running out of ideas for its right-slanted show. Only one idea got any ratings: "Angry White Men." This was the Fox News formula . . . but in TV, the inclination is imitation. In late January, *Donahue* offered "Angry White Men" Week—noisy debates dominated by B-listers from rightwing talk radio and far right groups. Monday was for railing against reparations for slavery, Tuesday for demands that English be designated our country's "official language," Wednesday for fuming about nonwhite immigrants and Thursday about affirmative action.

After a while, progressive guests weren't just outnumbered or outshouted—sometimes they were totally eliminated.

When rightwing talk radio host Neal Boortz complained that he'd been treated disrespectfully on the reparations program, he was granted his own hour, one-on-one with Phil. Boortz heavily promoted his upcoming appearance to his fans via radio and Internet. *Donahue* staffers were thrilled when the show got a good rating, but where was *Donahue*'s future if it based its growth on attracting the rightwing talk radio audience? Had Amy Goodman of *Democracy Now!* been featured solo for an hour on *Donahue* and promoted her rare, national TV appearance to her progressive base (which was swelling as war neared), the ratings may well have equaled Boortz's—and that kind of show offered growth potential.

On the immigration program, *Donahue* featured a guest too extreme even for Fox News. "Tonight," Phil opened, "we continue our debate with angry white men. And they appear to be everywhere, may I say. We're looking at how immigrants are impacting America." He then introduced his first guest (and his only guest for the first 10 minutes): Jared Taylor of American Renaissance, an articulate Yale graduate and leading figure in the white supremacist movement. Individuals who praise the confederacy and rail against "ugly Mexicans and ugly Haitians" don't generally get such a forum on national TV.

Weeks later, Taylor got an encore: a one-hour "Face-Off" with Phil. Although Phil denounced the extremist and ridiculed his wilder statements, Taylor's American Renaissance has long boasted of his two *Donahue* appearances—some of the best publicity the group ever received in mainstream media. AR is particularly proud of having been "part of Mr. Donahue's 'Angry White Men' series." On its website is a photo of Taylor across the table from Phil; MSNBC's on-screen banner reads, "Angry White Men—Keep Foreigners Out!"

★ ★ ★

I found it impossible to watch such fare. Phil had come out of retirement and I had joined him because we wanted to provide a forum for unheard voices and issues, not for racists. We wanted to be starmakers for progressives, to boost the careers and visibility of America's top peace and justice advocates. Instead, the show was doing wonders for the careers of some relatively obscure rightwing pundits and bigots. In the last two months of *Donahue*, rightwing radio ranter Steve Malzberg appeared seven times. Ted Koppel's *Nightline* had Kissinger as its ad-nauseam repeat guest; *Donahue* had Malzberg.

In January, I started working out of my home, doing what little work the show asked of me—about an hour a day. The main reason I didn't quit in protest was loyalty to Phil, who never gave up on turning the show around and regaining control. Another reason was that I had a one-year, no-cut contract—which meant I could work long hours behind-the-scenes as a pro bono consultant for antiwar efforts, while getting paid by GE for my labor.

The company, a military-industrial Goliath, was paying thousands of employees for war; shouldn't it pay one to work for peace?

## A DIFFICULT FACE FOR NBC

On Feb. 15, 2003, Bush's unrelenting push for war in Iraq prompted the biggest peace protests in world history, involving roughly 10 million people globally. In our country, almost a million people took part in antiwar events in 140 cities, reflecting the beliefs of millions more. Such a groundswell offered a solid base for a national TV show.

Ten days later, *Donahue* was cancelled.

MSNBC executives claimed publicly that the cause of the termination was simply poor ratings. To outsiders, this sounded plausible:

Donahue was an expensive show, and ratings were mediocre. But insiders knew that *Donahue*'s ratings were largely the result of management's constraints and control—and that it was still the most watched show on the low-rated channel.

The day after the cancellation, the outside world began to learn the truth about *Donahue*'s demise—thanks in part to an internal NBC report about MSNBC that was leaked to a TV industry website, AllYourTV.com.

NBC's internal report, never supposed to be made public, revealed serious anxiety about Phil Donahue in the network's hierarchy. Political anxiety. Anxiety about war critics. Written weeks before the show was cancelled, the document stated that Donahue represented *"a difficult public face for NBC in a time of war. . . . He seems to delight in presenting guests who are antiwar, anti-Bush and skeptical of the administration's motives."*

I'd always thought the role of journalism in a free society was to present diverse sources, including critics of officialdom—and that it was our patriotic duty to be skeptical, in times of peace or war. That view of journalism was clearly not shared by NBC News brass.

The NBC document went on to describe a nightmare scenario in which Donahue would become *"a home for the liberal antiwar agenda at the same time that our competitors are waving the flag at every opportunity."*

MSNBC's solution: Drop *Donahue*; pick up the flag.

If you watched MSNBC on the eve of war—with Phil fired and rightwingers hired—you know that MSNBC was second to no one in "waving the flag at every opportunity."

The prewar period offers a lesson: when journalists are so fervently waving the flag, they often lack the energy to do their jobs—to ask the tough questions before the bombs start dropping, before our young people are sent off to kill or be killed.

★ ★ ★

Just before Phil was sacked, MSNBC announced the hiring of the angriest white man, Michael Savage, to host a weekend show. The talk radio bigot had referred routinely to nonwhite countries as "turd world nations," dismissed child victims of gun violence as "ghetto slime," and said Latinos "breed like rabbits" and women "should have been denied the vote." He called the Million Mom March for gun control the "million dyke march." Our country, according to Savage, is a "she-ocracy where a minority of feminist zealots rule the culture"—with much of America "feminized and homosexualized." He called on antiwar leaders to be arrested in the event of an invasion of Iraq. All of this was well-known before MSNBC gave Savage his own cable news show—a step even Fox hadn't taken.

Hiring Savage sparked web satire.

Such a hiring decision required consultations with the entire network brass. The fact that Phil Donahue—who respects diverse guests and differing views—was deemed a "difficult public face for NBC," while Michael Savage was deemed a suitable face, says more about the myth of "The Liberal Media" than a dozen books could. It speaks volumes about the biases and terrors that dominate "mainstream" TV news.

Six days after Savage's hiring was announced, MSNBC's president emailed the staff to remind us all about mandatory "Diversity Workshops"—aimed at a work environment "where everyone is treated with respect" and embraces "the differences within MSNBC's own workforce." I skipped the workshop, figuring I could pick up the channel's current values by listening to its latest hire discuss "ghetto slime" and "dykes."

Savage would ultimately lose his MSNBC show when he referred to an apparently gay caller as a "sodomite" and told him, "You should only get AIDS and die, you pig." *Savage Nation* lasted four months, not quite as long as *Donahue*.

★ ★ ★

A week after exposing NBC's confidential report on his AllYour TV.com website, journalist Rick Ellis compiled a revealing *Donahue* postmortem based on internal emails and interviews with NBC/ MSNBC executives and producers. His account chronicled the fears and orders from Suitville that we on staff had encountered. Ellis wrote that anxiety mounted even before the show's launch.

In the two-plus months between Donahue's hiring and the debut of his show, there had been a marked shift in the way several high-ranking MSNBC executives looked at the program. That shift resulted in several early decisions about the mix of guests, decisions which by all accounts helped to sow the seeds of the show's ultimate collapse.

Network executives admitted to Ellis that there'd been "a directive aimed at the show." The directive imposed a "quota system on guests"—which often resulted in right-left shouting matches.

Almost from the beginning, there was a feeling among executives that "Donahue's political beliefs may be a problem." According to Ellis, executives admitted "to an early fear that Donahue may be a 'troublesome issue' as the U.S. moved closer to war in Iraq." (That NBC brass saw Phil as a "troublesome issue" is what I experienced from day 1.)

"Ironically," continued Ellis, "while liberals may have found the show's editorial mix unsatisfying, those inside the network often felt the show still leaned too far left for advertisers' comfort." By late August 2002, NBC executives were insisting on a more "centrist, women-friendly" show attractive to "the Middle American Silent Majority"—which Ellis noted is demographically "a tough sell" in cable news.

A focus group in October led to more pressure on Phil to tone down: Ellis quoted a network insider as saying that respondents thought he was "too combative" and made comments they considered "almost unpatriotic."

Ellis disclosed a smoking-gun email written by a network executive as the Iraq war approached: The advent of war would allow MSNBC to "reinvent itself" and take advantage of the "anticipated larger audience who will tune in during a time of war"—an opportunity to "cross-pollinate our programming" by placing network personalities throughout the wall-to-wall coverage. "It's unlikely," wrote the exec, "that we can use Phil in this way, particularly given his public stance on the advisability of the war effort."

There you have it. No room for a single dissenting voice. As we knew in our hearts all along: Even with big ratings, Phil was toast once the war neared.

⋆ ⋆ ⋆

Two days after *Donahue* was terminated, Sean Hannity interviewed CNN co-founder Reese Schonfeld and asked why MSNBC's bosses would "cancel their highest-rated show." Schonfeld replied, "They got afraid of the liberal tinge. . . . They listen to focus groups. They're desperate. They have no faith at all in their own editorial staff."

At hearing of *Donahue*'s demise, one of my regular MSNBC debating partners, a well-known conservative, actually complained to me that cable news was "becoming too rightwing."

## THE FOX EFFECT

With *Donahue* purged, *Countdown: Iraq* expanded to two hours per night, counting down even more breathlessly to war. Joe Scarborough started hosting a nightly MSNBC show featuring hawkish editorial attacks on "UN appeasers" and "the liberal media," and interviews with a conservative-tilted guest list—in an amateurish imitation of Fox's Bill O'Reilly.

When war came, most of corporate TV news did the Fox trot. Coverage was surreal, as if "talent" was auditioning for the highlight reel on Jon Stewart's *Daily Show*. As U.S. planes headed toward Baghdad on the war's opening night, Tom Brokaw hosted

O'Reilly impersonator?

various military analysts (with Gen. McCaffrey rosily predicting mass surrender by several Iraqi divisions). The NBC anchor turned to Dennis McGinn, the one admiral on his panel of generals.

> BROKAW: Admiral McGinn, one of the things that we don't want to do is destroy the infrastructure of Iraq, because in a few days we're going to own that country.
>
> MCGINN: Absolutely, Tom.

A few days later, a CNN anchor broke away from a news conference with an official of Saddam's government by explaining, "We're going to interrupt this press briefing right now because, of course, the U.S. government would disagree with most of what he is saying."

With shock-and-awe aerial bombardment causing civilian devastation in Baghdad, American TV networks repeatedly labeled them "surgical strikes." Jim Miklaszewski, NBC's reporter-in-residence at the Pentagon, crowed that "every weapon is precision guided—deadly accuracy designed to kill only the targets, not innocent civilians."

As U.S. troops advanced across the desert toward Baghdad, exhilarated embeds rode alongside tanks and armored vehicles and shouted their reports above the roar of the convoy—looking like unruly extras in a Mad Max movie.

On Fox News, there were so many bogus "discoveries" of Iraqi chemical and biological weapons that it's no wonder polling found many Fox viewers believing that WMD had actually been discovered.

Continuing its prewar track record, TV's wartime melodramas turned out to be hoaxes served up by deceptive official sources. We were told (with supporting video) that Private Jessica Lynch was "rescued" from torture by daring Special Forces after she'd heroically emptied her M-16 into Iraqi soldiers to avoid capture. In fact, as Lynch later explained, she never fired a shot and had been well treated by Iraqis. Moreover, U.S. "rescuers" encountered no resistance at the hospital where Lynch was found, since Iraqi soldiers were long gone. (Lynch's Iraqi medical attendants had actually tried to deliver her to a U.S. outpost but were fired on by U.S. troops.)

Even the toppling of Saddam's statue in the Baghdad square was largely staged. To this day, American television airs the footage as if it were the spontaneous act of jubilant Iraqis. A U.S. Army study has revealed that it was the work of U.S. Marines backed by army psychological warfare operatives, who rounded up Iraqi civilians to cheer. The idea to bring down the statue came from a U.S. Marine colonel.

★ ★ ★

Both MSNBC and Fox simply lifted the title of their 24-hour war coverage from the official name dreamt up by White House message-shapers: "Operation Iraqi Freedom." So much for journalistic independence. White House Press Secretary Ari Fleischer had initially called the invasion "Operation Iraqi Liberation," but the name had to be avoided due to its embarrassing acronym: OIL.

In many respects, MSNBC's war programming out-hawked Fox—with militantly pro-government coverage that won praise from rightwing media critics. In place of news, it offered celebratory montages of heroic soldiers and rejoicing Iraqis, ending in rousing slogans: "Home of the Brave" . . . "Let Freedom Ring." "MSNBC has patriotic flourishes throughout the day," reported the *New York Times*. "Along with the regular screen presence of an American flag, [President] Bush's portrait is featured on MSNBC's main set."

As predicted in the executive's email revealed by AllYourTV.com, a post-*Donahue* MSNBC was "reinventing itself" and using its expanded wartime audience as an opportunity to "cross-pollinate" network personalities. Michael Savage began appearing regularly on Scarborough's primetime show, where the tag team took turns spewing at traitors with enough gusto to make Fox blush. And their amorous on-screen "cross-pollinating" could make viewers blush:

SCARBOROUGH: Dr. Savage, welcome to our show.

SAVAGE: I'm honored to be on your show, Joe. I happen to love it. I think it's the best one on the air.

SCARBOROUGH: Other than yours. I saw yours last week; it was a great show.

On April 10, three weeks into the war which he portrayed as mission accomplished, Scarborough delivered a wacky commentary demanding that "disgraced" war skeptics like Jimmy Carter and Dennis Kucinich admit that "their wartime predictions were arrogant . . . misguided . . . and dead wrong." This on a show in which he spoke of Iraq possessing WMD. Scarborough was gleeful that antiwar "elitists" like Tim Robbins, Susan Sarandon, and Janeane Garofalo were facing cancellations and boycotts. Savage joined the conversation to say that "Hollywood idiots" are "absolutely committing sedition and treason."

Scarborough responded, "These leftist stooges for anti-American causes are always given a free pass. Isn't it time to make them stand up and be counted for their views?"

Noting MSNBC's rightwing antics, a *New York Times* piece stated that the channel "for the first time in years had a sense of momentum." The *Times* wrote that MSNBC chief Erik Sorenson was trying to differentiate his reporting "from what he called a mainstream style of automatic questioning of the government"—and quoted Sorenson: "After Sept. 11, the country wants more optimism and benefit of the doubt. . . . A big criticism of the mainstream press is that the beginning point is negative."*

MSNBC's jingo beat was cheered by rightwing journalism-basher Brent Bozell, who told the *Times*, "What Fox is doing, and frankly what MSNBC is also declaring by its product, is that one can be unabashedly patriotic and be a good news journalist at the same time."

★ ★ ★

Of course, MSNBC wasn't alone in imitating Fox. It was happening in much of TV. On CNN's morning show, Jack Cafferty was deployed as its resident pundit "with attitude."

JACK CAFFERTY: It's a red-letter day here in America. Air America, that communist radio network, starts broadcasting in a little while.

SOLEDAD O'BRIEN, ANCHOR: It's not communist.

CAFFERTY: It's not?

O'BRIEN: No.

CAFFERTY: Oh.

O'BRIEN: Liberal.

CAFFERTY: Well. Aren't they synonymous?

---

*Sorenson seemed to be echoing a cartoon character, *The Simpsons* anchor Kent Brockman, who famously apologized to the owner of the local nuclear plant, "This reporter promises to be more trusting and less vigilant in the future."

March 31, 2004, was indeed a red-letter day for America. A group of liberal and progressive investors had bought a small piece of the media rock, launching a talk radio network pitched to progressive-thinking people hungering for a voice in American broadcasting. And Air America took off.

What a novel concept: news-talk aimed at the other half of the political spectrum. The corporate suits of cable news wouldn't go near it. Timidity, ideology and corporatism were obstructing a marketplace of ideas.

You could blame it on fear of appearing liberal, on misguided patriotism, on advertisers. But don't blame Phil Donahue. He was willing to try. No one in cable news was willing to let him.

# EPILOGUE
## UNEMBEDDED

When I exited cable news, I felt disoriented and depressed. And then felt guilty about being depressed. After all, I hadn't entered television news with high expectations. I wasn't one of those TV news veterans who recalled "the good old days" under Murrow or Cronkite or whomever, and became disillusioned.

I'd never been *illusioned*.

In writing his book *The Jungle*, Upton Sinclair went undercover into Chicago's slaughterhouses, which apparently helped move him for a while to vegetarianism. When I entered the sausage factory of TV news, I was already a militant vegetarian, so to speak. I went in expecting to find timidity, censorship, tabloid lust, corporate skullduggery, and found them all . . . in spades.

So why did I leave so depressed? At CNN, where I was basically a guest, any progressive content I could get on national TV was a victory I felt good about. And at Fox News, I'd surpassed all expectations by appearing every week for years—building a base of viewers on enemy turf.

It was my brief yet intense tenure at MSNBC that left me with an excruciating sense of frustration I'd never felt before. When I started there in mid-2002, the stakes for our country were high, with the Bush regime exploiting the 9/11 catastrophe to promote its extreme and deceptive agenda. And each day I went off to work with the possibility that I could have some impact—debunk myths, expose wrongs, present eloquent opposing viewpoints in primetime—not only speak truth to power but actually be heard by the not-so-powerful. At a corporate TV network.

I was so close to actually having some media clout, and yet so far—and then step by step, I was pulled off stage and silenced by a news management terrified of reporting the news. As sophisticated as I was supposed to be about corporate censorship, there was a mad fleeting moment when I'd actually deluded myself into thinking that we could get away with truth-telling on a channel owned by General Electric.

During those weeks of temporary insanity at MSNBC, I felt in a small way like I imagined the original writers and cast at *Saturday Night Live* felt in 1975 as they were allowed to break the old rules of TV comedy. But TV news has stricter limits than comedy. And a war was coming. In no way would MSNBC obstruct the march to war. Indeed, it needed to be at the front of the march.

★ ★ ★

After my exile from cable news, I briefly became communications director for the antiwar presidential campaign of my friend Dennis Kucinich, the progressive congressman from Ohio. That campaign was an even bigger long shot than getting a principled Donahue show past NBC Suits. Although Kucinich was a leader in Congress against the Iraq war, the PATRIOT Act and corporate-drafted "free trade" deals, journalists would sometimes ask me for help pronouncing his last name. "Rhymes with spinach," I'd say, "and they're both good for you."

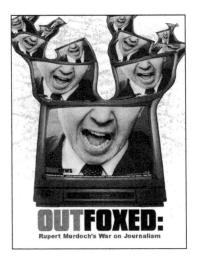

OUTFOXED:
Rupert Murdoch's War on Journalism

Early in 2004, filmmaker Robert Greenwald started leaning on me to be a whistle-blower in his *Outfoxed* exposé of Fox News and corporate media in general. I was at first reluctant, hoping I might still find a home somewhere in TV punditry. But I decided to appear in *Outfoxed* to blast both Fox and MSNBC. More people recognize me from that insurgent documentary than all my TV appearances combined.

As for Phil Donahue, MSNBC drove him off nightly TV, but not off the public stage. He continues to speak out passionately for U.S. withdrawal from Iraq, for war veterans, for reform of our corporatized media system.

★ ★ ★

The three cable news channels carry on even more tawdry and tabloid and ranting than before—with Fox News veering ever rightward for a primetime audience that roughly doubles the audience of conformist CNN and is several times that of clueless MSNBC.

Changes in "talent" at the news channels resemble musical chairs on the *Titanic*. Especially at MSNBC, which was once exhorted by GE CEO Jeff Immelt to attract as much attention as Fox News, even if it meant having "clowns jumping out of airplanes." No clowns have been hired, but MSNBC did lure Rita Cosby and her tabloid circus away from Fox.

MSNBC's right tilt continued. When CNN cancelled *Crossfire*, MSNBC scooped up its co-host, Tucker Carlson, to host his own show. Few watch the bow-tied conservative on MSNBC, despite attention-getting ploys like actually applauding terrorism: "Twenty years ago," declared Carlson, "[France] blew up the Greenpeace ship, the *Rainbow Warrior*, in Auckland Harbor. It was a bold and good thing to do." Days later, he called it "something all Frenchmen can be proud of." Explosives planted by French secret service agents killed a man aboard the ship, which had sailed in protests of France's nuclear tests in the Pacific. A "bold and good" murder.

Though he remained the Suits' top dog at MSNBC, Chris Matthews often seemed to be auditioning for a job at Fox. Near the beginning of 2006, he compared Michael Moore to Osama bin Laden, quoted "the wonderful Michael Savage" about *Brokeback Mountain*, and remarked that everybody, including Matthews, likes President Bush "except for the real whack jobs maybe on the left."

Appearing out of place at MSNBC is former sports guy Keith Olbermann, perhaps the most independent voice in cable news; he once asserted in a C-SPAN interview that there are executives at NBC "who do not like to see the current presidential administration criticized at all."

At the end of 2005, a momentous day occurred in cable news history: CNN went dark on the Prince of Darkness, Bob Novak. My former *Crossfire* foe lost his pundit seat at the network he'd been with since its founding in 1980. CNN let Novak go after he blew a fuse during a live debate, cursed, ripped off his mike and walked off the set. Don't feel bad for Novak; he became a Fox News pundit.

And don't feel bad for CNN; it replaced Novak with former Fox pundit Bill Bennett, known both for his moralizing conservatism and his big-time gambling habit. Shortly before CNN hired Bennett, he had bizarrely declared on his radio talkshow that "you could abort every black baby in this country, and your crime rate would go down"—adding that it would be "morally reprehensible." In addition to Bennett, CNN hired Clear Channel talk-radio blowtorch Glenn Beck, known for wishing violent death upon Michael Moore and Dennis Kucinich, and for calling Cindy Sheehan a "big prostitute."

Cable news has become a downwardly spiraling circle: three dogs chasing each other's tails to the right.

## THE GOOD NEWS

Not long after I closed the door behind me on TV news, my spirits lifted as I witnessed a mass awakening, a profound shift in thought and action among liberals, progressives and just plain independent thinkers—with millions of people no longer willing to accept the media status quo.

I'd founded FAIR in 1986 with the motto "Don't Take the Media Lying Down." Over the years, we built a respected nonprofit with a loyal, ever-expanding base of support—but nothing close to a mass movement.

By 2003, something was in the air, much of it due to the Iraq war. Conventional wisdom would portray the war as an "intelligence failure," but many Americans saw it as a *media failure*—the result of a commercial media system in bed with official sources, intimidated by conservatives, allergic to genuine debate. As the war approached, Americans assiduously sought alternatives, turning to the BBC and international sources, to independent websites and blogs, to progressive outlets that experienced unparalleled growth.

NBC's smoldering gun memo that doomed *Donahue*—fretting that the show would allow dissent while "our competitors are waving the flag at every opportunity"—got decent mainstream coverage. (I pushed it to every TV writer I knew.) It was even bigger news on the Internet and independent media.

Then at the apex of anger aimed at corporate media, word got out—largely via the Net—about a dirty backroom deal: The same media conglomerates that had obstructed news and debate as the Bush team deceptively sold a war were being rewarded by Bush's Federal Communications Commission with rule changes allowing media whales to get still fatter. Network news had silenced opposing views while Colin Powell pushed for war at the United Nations. Now Powell's son Michael, the FCC chair appointed by Bush, was moving to scrap the few remaining rules against conglomeration. And Michael Powell had the nerve to praise the "thrilling" TV coverage of the war in justifying his gift to the media titans.*

The 2003 uprising against the FCC was unprecedented in U.S. history—the biggest mobilization ever on an issue of media policy. More than a million letters and emails of protest flooded the FCC, crashing its email system. This time the mobilizers went beyond FAIR and veteran media reformers; Internet powerhouses like MoveOn.org joined in. A new reform group Free Press played a lead role, as did Common Cause—along with Consumers Union and labor unions. Even the National Rifle Association and conservative groups piled on.

In one afternoon, congressional phone lines were overloaded by tens of thousands of calls urging a vote to overturn the FCC's new rules. And Congress did. The FCC was ultimately thwarted in federal court, with the court citing the public outcry in its decision.

Another explosion occurred on the eve of the 2004 election, when conservative Sinclair Broadcast Group—owner of 60 TV stations, more than any other company—ordered its stations to air a "news" special drawn from a partisan Kerry-bashing movie. Sinclair's Washington bureau chief called it "biased political propaganda." An Internet campaign arose overnight to challenge Sinclair's use of the public airwaves

---

*Corporate radio giants Clear Channel (1,200 stations) and Cumulus (300 stations) also aided the war effort by using their outlets to organize pro-war rallies, at which the Dixie Chicks were targets of vilification—because of a quip about President Bush made by the band's lead singer. Some Clear Channel stations stopped playing their songs; Cumulus banned them for a while on its 42 country stations. At a rally organized by a Cumulus station in Louisiana, spectators cheered as a 15-ton tractor smashed piles of Dixie Chicks CDs.

to campaign for its chosen candidate. The protest rocked the company's stock price and advertisers. Sinclair retreated.

In 2005, there were still more media-activist upsurges, online and off, to challenge White House propaganda efforts—such as payola pundits like Armstrong Williams; fake news segments planted in local news; GOP operatives planted at White House briefings. In 2006, progressive blogs challenged conservative media bias like never before.

These media mobilizations took my breath away. My only regret was that such a potent movement had not coalesced by 2002—to flex its muscles against MSNBC brass in defense of an unfettered *Donahue*.

★   ★   ★

In May 2005, Free Press and an invigorated media reform movement brought 2,700 activists to St. Louis to plot local and national strategies toward diversifying the media system. Some goals:

- Break up media monopolies through antitrust enforcement, and expand minority and nonprofit ownership.

- Create genuine public broadcasting funded by an independent trust—replacing the current corrupt system financed by business interests and a rightwing-run, taxpayer-funded Corporation for Public Broadcasting.

- Preserve and expand public access on cable TV; nonprofit channels on cable and satellite TV; low power radio; low-cost, high-speed community Internet.*

One of my favorite media reforms, proposed by economist Dean Baker and Free Press founder Robert McChesney, would allow citizens to redirect $150 of their federal taxes to the nonprofit media outlets of their choice. Such a content-neutral reform could bolster diverse

---

*As Jeff Chester of the Center for Digital Democracy warns, the free and open Internet we're accustomed to is at risk because big phone and cable companies who sell us high-speed access have lobbied and won key regulatory changes. They long for a privately-controlled Internet that charges a fee for, and monitors, "our every move in cyberspace"—while pushing nonmonetary communications into the slow lanes. Only an active citizenry will ensure that Congress blocks their efforts to turn the superhighway into a toll road.

media alternatives to the tune of billions of dollars per year. Currently, the biggest media subsidies go to the Murdochs and GEs and Sinclairs who get monopoly broadcast licenses and control of the public's airwaves (worth billions) virtually for free.

★ ★ ★

The growth of the media reform movement is an inspiration. But it faces one of Washington's most powerful lobbies, representing corporations that heavily shape the images voters have of their elected officials. The media lobby has historically backed both Republicans and corporate Democrats like Bill Clinton, but lately it has grown closer to the GOP. In September 2005, the chief of staff to Republican leader Tom DeLay became a top lobbyist for Time Warner, while the head lobbyist for Disney/ABC was an active Republican who used to lobby for Murdoch.

During the 2004 election, CEO Sumner Redstone of Viacom/CBS spoke for many media moguls when he publicly endorsed Bush: "A Republican administration is better for media companies than a Democratic one." Explained Redstone, "The Republican administration has stood for many things we believe in, deregulation and so on."

## BECOME THE MEDIA

The most exciting trend in the media world has been the growth of dynamic, independent outlets. It's been fueled on the demand side by an epic migration of discerning news consumers away from corporate fare. And on the supply side, by a can-do attitude that proclaims, "Don't just criticize the media—become the media."

Thank God (and Al Gore) for the Internet, which has radically changed the way millions of us give and get the news. Websites such as CommonDreams, AlterNet, Buzzflash and ZNet, to name just a few, have boomed in recent years. 2002 saw the birth of left-leaning blogs like *DailyKos*, *Eschaton* and Tom Tomorrow's *This Modern World* that now get millions of visitors. *HuffingtonPost.com* has taken off. The right dominates TV punditry and talk radio, but progressives have trounced conservatives in using the Internet to organize, fundraise and disseminate information. That progressives have taken so quickly to this new, more interactive medium demonstrates how powerful was their alienation from old-line media.

And the Internet has allowed alternative marketing of documentaries. Without the backing of a movie studio or TV network, Robert Greenwald has reached a mass audience with his documentaries thanks to Internet marketing in alliance with grassroots organizations. *Outfoxed* was Amazon.com's top-selling DVD when it was released in 2004, outselling major Hollywood releases.

Another booming media project is the award-winning *Democracy Now!*, hosted by Amy Goodman and Juan Gonzalez. From its origins as Pacifica Radio's morning show, *DN!* has grown into the largest public media collaboration in the United States with hundreds of outlets on radio (Pacifica and NPR affiliates) and TV (public access, PBS affiliates and satellite), plus the Internet. It is seen via satellite thanks to

two independent channels—Free Speech TV and Link TV—that carry bold current affairs programming unthinkable on corporate networks.

Breaking the rightwing monopoly in AM talk radio has been Air America and its affiliates. After some early financial missteps, the radio network expanded while conservative talk stagnated.

A combination of Bushnoia and Internet marketing has propelled independent magazines—*Mother Jones*, *The Nation* and others—to record highs in paid circulation. ("Bush is bad for the country," the saying goes, "but great for *The Nation*.") The mushrooming of independent book pub-

Amy Goodman of *Democracy Now!*

lishers is another sign that free-thinking consumers are getting serious about feeding their heads.

If you've read this far, dear reader, I suspect that you'd love an alternative to CNN, Fox and MSNBC. Launching a TV news network will not be easy. But an effort is underway toward such a network— called "The Real News"—led by Paul Jay, formerly with CBC in Toronto. The goal is to broadcast a nightly news show on digital cable, satellite and web, and expand from there. The network is to be free of advertising and corporate or government funding. Inspired by the online fundraising success of MoveOn and the Howard Dean campaign, The Real News plans to raise capital through small contributions from many thousands of donors. It would then hire top journalists and unleash them on real news, real debates, real goings-on in Washington. It would leave shark attacks and celebrity trials to CNN, Fox and MSNBC.

★ ★ ★

Nowadays I tend to speak of "corporate media" vs. "independent media." I prefer that paradigm over "mainstream media" vs. "alternative media"—because I dislike the implication that *alternative* media are secondary and focus on marginal issues or causes. Today's corporate media, especially cable news, focus so tenaciously on the marginal and trivial, on the Gary Condits and runaway brides, that it's hardly "news," mainstream or otherwise. And when corporate media do cover important subjects like war or politics, they have an uncanny ability to obsess on the petty, on news as soap opera, while missing the core of the story.

That's why—on big issues of war and peace, global economy, social justice, environment, civil rights and Constitutional liberties—active citizens are flocking to serious independent outlets and blogs that cover these crucial topics with passion, depth and detail. Independent media are "unbought and unbossed." You may wonder about their biases or limited resources, but you never worry that corporate owners, agendas or sponsors are obstructing the flow of information.

It's no accident that corporate news is so often empty and denatured—any more than it's an accident that supermarket white bread is sold minus the germ and bran. News is rendered nutritionless when it's a processed product brought to market by distant and soulless corporations.

Listen to Lowry Mays, CEO of radio colossus Clear Channel, as he tells *Fortune* magazine that he cares about ad sales, not program quality: "If anyone said we were in the radio business, it wouldn't be someone from our company. We're not in the business of providing news and information. We're not in the business of providing well-researched music. We're simply in the business of selling our customers products."

Or listen to Viacom's president, formerly an ad salesman, when asked by a reporter a few years ago about the most exciting trend in TV programming: "Why are you bothering me about programming? I don't watch shows, and I don't pick the programs. . . . The most exciting trend in programming is the cash flow we make. The shows that are financially successful are the ones that excite me."

In independent media, it's content that matters. An end in itself. Not a means to sell ads or make easy profits. When the staff of *Democracy Now!* seizes hold of a story—whether about war atrocities or corporate abuse or repression of activists—you get thoroughness, factual rigor and heart and soul. You don't get O'Reilly-style bluster. You don't get sleaze or tease to hold you through the next commercial. You don't get a corporate suit telling journalists to back off or tone down.

When Upton Sinclair went inside meatpacking plants to write *The Jungle,* his book convinced many Americans to give up meat. Having been inside the TV news sausage factory, I can wholeheartedly recommend that you find alternatives to corporate-processed news.

Independent media persevere without big sponsors. All they have is their diligence and your support.

You have the power to see that they thrive.

# ACKNOWLEDGMENTS

This book centers on my personal account of what I saw, heard and learned in and around cable news. It's my perspective, told as fairly and accurately as possible—based on my memory of events. Memory can be spotty; where possible, I've relied on contemporaneous notes, emails, transcripts and tapes. This is not an "objective" report derived from interviewing a variety of sources. I know that others, especially the Suits criticized in these pages, will have different perspectives on these same events—"disgruntled" . . . "exaggerated" . . . "Jeff who?"

My goal has been to neither overstate nor understate the problems of TV news, but to recount my experiences with nuance and contradiction. My very presence inside these channels was a contradiction—proving that corporate TV is not monolithic and that rules often have exceptions.

TV show dialogue comes from tapes—or from network-provided transcripts, which are not 100 percent accurate. (On one show in which I plugged my book on "Limbaugh's Reign of Error," it was originally transcribed as "Reign of *Terror*.") In some dialogue, I've removed repetitions, false starts and stutters—what would be considered audio typos.

★ ★ ★

This book could not have been written without the support of others. For their patience, I thank my long-suffering daughters—Sequoia ("Stic") and Cassidy ("Cady")—and their even longer-suffering mom, Stephanie Kristal.

My parents, Sol and Viola Cohen, have always stood by me despite a string of public embarrassments—much like our current president's parents (though my failures, thankfully, weren't so public or massive). Ditto for my loyal brothers Steve and Ron; Ron is an expert in socially-conscious investing and manages my . . . ahem . . . finances.

Thanks to friends and colleagues who read chapters of the manuscript and provided feedback: Norman Solomon, Jim Naureckas, Martin Lee, Mira Ptacin, Bob Katz, Peter Hart, Steve Rendall and a couple insiders who must remain nameless. At their behest, I deleted some items, usually tasteless humor. If you end up reading those juicy parts in a sequel after this book becomes a bestseller, blame them. Better yet, blame the nameless guys. Blaming unnamed sources is now a media ritual.

I am indebted to tireless researcher Mira Ptacin, who reviewed so many tapes of my TV debates that I suspect she started rooting for the rightwingers. If there are mistakes of fact in this fact-filled book, blame her. As for errors of interpretation, don't fault Mira—it's those nameless guys referred to earlier.

This book wouldn't exist if not for FAIR and its topnotch staff: Hillary Goldstein, Peter Hart, Sanford Hohauser, Julie Hollar, Janine Jackson, Jim Naureckas, Steve Rendall, Deborah Thomas. And FAIR might not exist if not for the clumsy political spying of the LAPD. Thank you, Chief Gates.

For their years of friendship and support, I'm grateful to Liz Iler, Hollie Ainbinder, Crystal Zevon and Sam Husseni. Thanks to my nephew and computer genius Muir Cohen, for keeping me online, if not in line; to Eldad Benary, for grabbing photos off videos; to Deborah Thomas, for help with graphics; to Gabriel Voiles, for my website at jeffcohen.org; and to my lawyers on the book, Ken Swezey and Lisa Digernes.

My gratitude extends to everyone at PoliPointPress. They've worked their tails off on this book every step of the way. Of course, these words are being written well in advance of that final step: sales.

Finally, I must salute the Woodstock Wednesday Night Poker Club for their support and the extra cash that sustained me during those lean months before the advance arrived.

# CREDITS

Cartoons by Matt Wuerker: pages 16, 86, and 190.

Cartoons by Tom Tomorrow: pages 34, 70, and 116.

Photo on page 54: AP Photo/Richard Drew.

Cartoon on page 92 by Walt Handelsman, *Newsday* © Tribune Media Services, Inc. All Rights Reserved. Reprinted with permission.

Cartoon on page 103 by John Branch (*San Antonio Express-News*).

Cartoon on page 109 by Clay Butler, Capitola, CA.

Graphic on page 124 from *You Back the Attack! We'll Bomb Who We Want! Remixed War Propaganda* by Micah Ian Wright (Seven Stories, 2003).

Photo on page 126 by REUTERS/Gleb Garanich.

Cartoon on page 128 by Kirk Anderson, St. Paul, MN.

Cartoon on page 137 by Joel Pett (*Lexington Herald-Leader*).

Photo on page 144 by AP Photo/Nick Ut.

Web graphic on page 187 by www.patriotboy.blogspot.com.

Cartoon on page 199 by Toles © 2003 *The Washington Post*. Reprinted with permission of UNIVERSAL PRESS SYNDICATE. All rights reserved.

Photo on page 202 by Chet Gordon.

# INDEX

# ABOUT THE AUTHOR

Jeff Cohen is the founder of FAIR, the progressive media watch group based in New York. He devolved from media critic to media pundit, appearing regularly on national TV—including as a co-host of *Crossfire* on CNN, a weekly panelist on Fox News and a daily commentator on MSNBC.

He was senior producer of MSNBC's *Donahue* until the show was terminated on the eve of the Iraq war. He is the co-author of a number of books, including *Wizards of Media Oz* and *The Way Things Aren't: Rush Limbaugh's Reign of Error*. Cohen's columns have run in many publications, including the *Los Angeles Times, USA Today, Washington Post, Atlanta Constitution, Miami Herald, Brill's Content, The Nation*, and many other publications.

Before founding FAIR, he worked in Los Angeles as an ACLU lawyer. In 2003, he was communications director of the Kucinich for President campaign. He writes and lectures widely about media and politics, reachable through jeffcohen.org.

He lives in upstate New York, where he helps raise two smart, beautiful daughters.

# OTHER BOOKS FROM
# PoliPointPress

**Nomi Prins,** *Jacked: How "Conservatives" Are Picking Your Pocket—Whether You Voted for Them or Not*
Relates the major political issues of our time to each card in your wallet, linking the current administration's record to everyday household concerns.
ISBN: 0-9760621-8-6 $12.95, soft cover.

*The Blue Pages: A Directory of Companies Rated by Their Politics and Practices*
Helps consumers make conscious buying decisions using their political and social values.
ISBN: 0-9760621-1-9 $9.95, soft cover.

**Steven Hill,** *10 Steps to Repair American Democracy*
Identifies the key problems with American democracy and proposes ten specific reforms to reinvigorate it.
ISBN: 0-9760621-5-1 $11.00, soft cover.

**Yvonne Latty,** *In Conflict: Iraq War Veterans Speak Out on Duty, Loss, and the Fight to Stay Alive*
Features the unheard voices, extraordinary experiences, and personal photographs of a broad mix of Iraq War veterans.
ISBN: 0-9760621-4-3 $24.00, hard cover.

**Joe Conason,** *The Raw Deal: How the Bush Republicans Plan to Destroy Social Security and the Legacy of the New Deal*
Describes the well-financed and determined effort to undo the Social Security Act and New Deal programs.
ISBN: 0-9760621-2-7 $11.00, soft cover.

**John Sperling et al.,** *The Great Divide: Retro vs. Metro America*
Explains why our nation is so bitterly divided into what the authors call Retro and Metro America.
ISBN: 0-09760621-0-0 $19.95, soft cover.

For more information, please visit www.p3books.com.